Living
Midnight

Three Movements of the Tao

by
Jan Fries

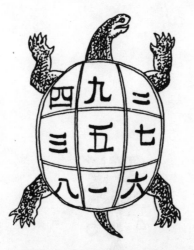

The square of nine chambers

Published by
Mandrake of Oxford
PO Box 250
OXFORD
OX1 1AP (UK)

A CIP catalogue record for this book is available from the British Library and the US Library of Congress.

ISBN 1 869928 504

Contents

Dedicated to Chang Kuo Lau´s immortal donkey
and the donkey in us all.

Acknowledgements

While books generally tend to fall from the sky and manifest first in dreams and then in an overwhelming obsessive urge to manifest on paper, this one happened almost by accident. An old text on the eight signs was rewritten and expanded so much in the process that it threatened to become a small book. To improve on this dismal state two other essays were written. I wish to thank the spirits who appeared and asked for a place on paper. Then there are those who supported the writing with encouragement, literary references, wild questions and new ideas. I wish to thank Astrid Bauer, K.-P. v. d. Eltz, Kenneth Grant, Julia, Kim Da Ga Nee, Mogg Morgan of Mandrake, Nema, Denny Sargent, and Gavin Semple for their unique contributions. If you find errors in this text I can assure you that they are of my own making and must be good for something one way or another. Finally, I would like to add a cheerful Thank You to all readers.

1   Pa Kua - Eight Signs

Divination and magick in ancient China

Let's start this nice and easy. Our topic is not entirely simple, and so we might as well enjoy those brief and passing moments of innocence, they'll soon disappear when ignorance is replaced by all-out confusion. Not bad for a start, as confusion is just the state we need if we want to understand something new. We begin with a voidness that is so empty that it contains nothing, not even itself. Out of this absence, something appears. It is still a bit chaotic, but there it is. Out of something the two aspects of duality arise and balance each other. The two became three. The three turn into five, and five transform the world. Five become eight, eight increase into sixty-four and sixty-four give birth to the ten-thousand things that make up the world we all experience. With the ten-thousand things we leave the realm of mystical cosmology and enter daily life. You know what things I'm talking about. Some of them pile up in front of bookshelves, in dark corners of rooms and in deep drawers or way up in the attic. Others cluster in your bag, hide when you need them and reappear quite innocently as soon as you've decided to do without them. Some of them don't really work and all of them want a bit of attention to brighten up their existence. Then there are the things that grow in places and others that wriggle or fly around and buzz. Most of the ten-thousand things have a mind of their own. Some of them are really big and noisy and go past in a hurry. Some things may come after you, some come to fill your belly and some will remain when you are gone. And they just wait for you to come back. Welcome to the world! Here are the ten-thousand things and you are welcome to them. While this may not sound especially mystical it may give you a good idea why it may be a relief to return to simplicity.

Oracular roots

Ancient Chinese literature includes a gem of the first order. It is the venerable *I Ching* (Yijing) that, making use of the simple interplay of two signs, produces eight magical symbols, the *Pa Kua* (Ba Gua) which combine to create sixty-four images that represent the entire scope of changes in our universe. Of course a vocabulary of sixty-four images does not seem very extensive when we have to express the totality of the world's phenomena with it. Luckily the sixty-four images are not on their own. It's when they get into contact with your brain that the magick begins.

> *The Book of Changes contains the measure of heaven and earth; therefore it enables us to comprehend the Tao of heaven and earth and its order.*

Thus speaks the great treatise, the *Ta Chuan*, and these words are not an exaggeration. A book that describes all the possible transformations in the world is not necessarily easy reading. Luckily, most of it is not even meant to be read. In fact, if you only read the *I Ching* there are quite a lot of subtle changes you won't notice, as your mind will be focused in the wrong direction. *The Book of Changes* is an oracle and its primary use is divination. Consider the way that oracles work.

To divine the unknown is not just a matter of asking a question and receiving an answer. The moment you sit down to ask your question, the world seems to hold its breath. Divination tends to change the mind, and your understanding of a situation. As you are part of the situation, and influence it from the instant your awareness enters into the game, a change in your awareness equals a change in the world. What is this

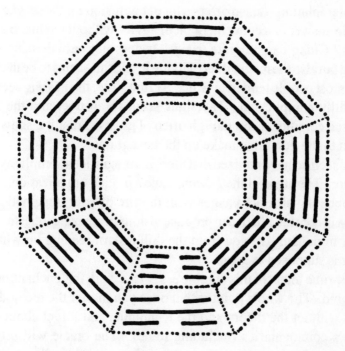

Double circle of primal and later heaven, inner circle = primal heaven, outer circle = later heaven. The trigrams are seen from inside the circle.

world, after all, but your belief in it? And while we are at it, what are you but a focus of belief?

To divine is to bind and influence the pattern of events, and this is the case with all oracles, even the most silly and playful ones. To ask a question and to receive an answer is to transform the world you believe in. This is an act of magick, but it is not the only one. A good oracle should be able to provide a fitting answer. This implies that each system of divination requires a vocabulary to give answers in, and to describe as much of the world, and your consciousness of it, as possible.

Each oracular method is a mirror of yourself and all otherness. To understand an oracle is to understand its cosmology. Here the *I Ching*, with its blend of simplicity and refined differentiation offers much food for contemplation. It also offers a lot of confusion for those who want a simple answer or a convenient bit of advice without too much effort.

The *I Ching* can be quite tricky. It does not only demand some reading but also the magical act of living it, and this seems to be the point where most people tend to give up. At first sight, the *I Ching* seems to be awfully complicated. The signs seem so abstract and the time-honoured commentaries, though often of great originality, show little relation to the items that make up the hexagrams.

Few seem to have realized that there is a magnificent simplicity to its structure. The signs of the *I Ching* have a hidden organization. Once you imbue the abstract images with the fire of your imagination the oracle will come to life. It can produce visions of amazing intensity right in your mind and free you from the dull task of reading up what the answer is supposed to mean.

The prime intent of this humble essay is to work this enchantment in your mind. The whole point is that once you master the method, you can do without the theory and the technique, and forget about other people's commentaries (including mine). The oracle will produce answers, in the shape of vision and imagination, that will suit exactly your nature and understanding of the world.

Do I hear you complaining that this seems like an awfully hard task? Come on, you didn't think that magick would be easy, did you? Let me surprise you. It's a lot easier than you ever guessed. Good divination should be both easy and natural. If you require effort and strain to do the job, there's something wrong. I don't ask you to believe me. It's much more worthwhile to do the imagination exercises and convince yourself that you can do it.

The origin of the I Ching

Let us now take a look at the supposed origin of the *I Ching*. Keep an open mind and doubt as much as you like. If you have any preconceptions on the topic you may remember to forget them for a while. If you know better, let me congratulate you. I am no sinologist and haven't lived in China for centuries. As a barbarian who likes to go for forest walks my main interest is to offer a useful method of doing things practically. I apologize for any errors that may lurk in this text. The odd bit of misinformation can hardly be avoided as Chinese magick and religion are highly obscure topics. For a start, Westerners are rarely given all the required information. For another, Taoists themselves come in a wide range of cults, sects and movements. Many of these groups are at odds with each other where it comes to the proper interpretation of symbols or the way to perform a ritual. There is a great deal of secrecy involved in Chinese magick.

In these matters one can often observe two forces at work. One is the force of tradition. Many Taoists feel highly committed to keep their rituals and meditations in close accord with traditional teachings, and the older they are the better. This sort of behaviour produced a rather creative fashion of writing history. Chinese historians have always sought to portray a past as it ought to have been, and frequently recent innovations in custom were attributed to much earlier periods. The same sort of thing happened in Taoist ritual. Where old age means status, each sect had to produce a lineage leading to remote antiquity.

On the other hand there is the fact that there are plenty of different schools of Taoism around. According to F. Stockwell (1993) there are eighty-six Taoist sects. Though they all have a certain commitment to the writings of the early sages, the way they interpret the sacred texts and the rituals and practices they perform show a wide range of innovative experiment. Each school or sect began with one or several persons who decided to found their own tradition. This is the other force, we could call it creative innovation. In order to blend tradition and innovation, new customs were often attributed to prehistory or accepted as they supposedly came from some venerable spirit or deity.

The result is a living tradition, a range of systems that survive as they adapt to new world views and circumstances. Consequently, this book combines several sorts of traditional lore with innovative methods of making things easier. I hope that my readers, especially those who happen to be Chinese Taoists, will forgive this adventurous undertaking. The theory and storytelling are mainly there to divert your attention, to confuse your conscious mind and to give suggestions to the deep. What will you make out of them?

That *I Ching* literature is so extensive can't be helped. The oldest known commentaries on the system are said to come from Ji Chang, also known as Prince Wen (c.1150 BCE) who wrote them in his spare time. He had more than enough of that, as the tyrant Chou Hsin had exiled and imprisoned him. No doubt the prince often made use of the *I Ching* in his captivity, and kept asking questions on his fate and the length of his stay. To consult an oracle is to change the mind. The *I Ching*, then as now a reliable way of sorting out the mind, gave him a full total of 64 different answers, most of them boiling down to a cheerful 'be patient, you old fool'.

Prince Wen, in his amazement that there could be so many ways of counselling patience, decided to write an extensive commentary on the good book. During the process, he used his educated poetic style to the limit and became an expert at biding his time. The oracle had told him that his exile would last for seven years, and of course, this turned out to be accurate. Also, noble people had pretty comfortable prisons in those days. Though he occasionally worried if he would lose his head, he did not have to worry where the next meal came from. His literary work consisted of a few brief lines which commented on the nature of each hexagram.

Prince Wen's son Ji Fa, the Duke of Chou, named himself King Wu and managed to overthrow the tyrant Chou Hsin. He gave the title 'King' to his father posthumously and started his own dynasty. He also edited his father's work and expanded on it. He had a slightly more cheerful outlook on life but refrained from letting it show. We

The death of Hun Tun

owe to him the commentaries on the lines, many of which show great originality. When he published the texts he gave them the title *Chou -I*, meaning *The Changes Of Chou*. In Chinese legend, both King Wen and his son, King Wu, had a reputation for unworldy holiness. According to the famous novel *Creation of the Gods*, they made much use of the *I Ching* and were celebrated as just rulers chosen by heaven to overthrow the Shang dynasty. The term '*Chou-I*' refers to the fact that the *I Ching* became popular with the start of the Chou dynasty.

Since those early days, *The Book of Changes* was edited, corrected, rephrased and transformed by dozens of (usually anonymous) authors. Even those passages which used to be ascribed to King Wen and his son show the influence of later hands when analysed linguistically. It was translated into various dialects and languages, so that the work you see on the bookshelf today is a far cry from the original manuscript that King Wen composed over a cup of good wine. As a result, the full *I Ching* including its various commentaries has grown to formidable size.

Each of the 64 signs has come to have a lot of meanings, and if you only rely on literature to receive your answer, you'll find something useful in each of them, provided you keep reading for long enough. While this may suffice to satisfy the fluffy-minded, or those careless souls who use divination to confirm their preconceptions, I am sure you are made from different wood and want nothing less than an in-depth treatment of the topic.

Luckily, the *I Ching* was not invented by imprisoned nobles, but by practical minded visionaries and lunatics like you and me. This makes it easier to use and develop in a creative spirit. Keep in mind that we are not dealing with a monument but with a practical working tool. It might even be proposed that all texts of the *I Ching* are commentaries. The original 'book' consisted only of the signs. Better still, there may be a hidden structure to it. Cheer up! It furthers to cross the great water, especially using a boat.

The Green Emperor Fu-Hsi

In the beginning

The origin of the *I Ching* corresponds to Taoist cosmology. The beginning of the world, if this term may be used at all, was not an act of creation in the early myths and philosophies. Think of it as a process of becoming. Out of nothing arose the Hun Tun, the primal undifferentiated chaos. This can be considered an abstract concept, but it also had a mythical form. Early myths (given in the *Shanhaijing*) describe the Hun Tun as a birdlike monstrosity, a fearless being with four wings and six feet which feeds on fish and likes to dance. Its body is supposed to look a bit like a sack and its face is absent. In a philosophical sense the Hun Tun may be represented by such concepts as Not Yet and No More. Or forget about the concepts, as this being of the beginning is older than anything that can be thought of. Undying and unborn, the Hun Tun travels the spaceways in the realm of no difference.

Chuang Tsu expanded on these concepts. In his writings, the Hun Tun lacks a face and any of the openings that humans have to sense the world. Self-contained to the utmost degree, the primal chaos had no means of sensing otherness. To help it out of its simple state, light and darkness decided to drill seven holes into the Hun Tun. Through these holes, the senses began to assimilate the world, and when all seven were present, the Hun Tun died.

This may give you an idea why so much of Taoist meditation is focused on seeing without seeing, hearing without hearing, feeling without feeling, and forgetting oneself on the way. Quite simply, the Taoist ceases to pay attention to the outer and the inner universe, and returns to the primal state of the Hun Tun. The end of this process is not at the end, and of course nobody ever gets there. Be that as it may, and it usually is, in the beginning of time out of the whirling spiral of the Hun Tun, the primal polarity was born. This polarity received the names yin and yang, two terms which have been badly abused by the new age movement.

0 1 2 3 4 5 6 7

8 9 10 11 12 13 14 15

16 17 18 19 20 21 22 23

24 25 26 27 28 29 30 31

32 33 34 35 36 37 38 39

40 41 42 43 44 45 46 47

48 49 50 51 52 53 54 55

56 57 58 59 60 61 62 63

The Fu Hsi arrangement

Binary code:

0=0	7=111	14=1110	21=10101
1=1	8=1000	15=1111	22=10110
2=10	9=1001	16=10000	23=10111
3=11	10=1010	17=10001	etc
4=100	11=1011	18=10010	
5=101	12=1100	19=10011	
6=110	13=1101	20=10100	

The Yin and the Yang

Originally, the word *yin* meant the shady side (of a mountain) while *yang* referred to the sunny side. These metaphors are surprisingly precise in their flexibility. For a start, the placement of light and shadow depends very much on the season and the time of day. For another, yin and yang were thought of in an abstract way relating to the energetic state of biosystems. These concepts had little to do with such later interpretations as 'life/death', 'strong/weak', 'male/female' or worse yet, 'good/evil'. The inventors of the yin and yang concept had good reason to keep their symbols so abstract. Can you think of any?

It is the foundation of early Chinese cosmology that yin and yang together assume form in the T'ai Chi (T'aiji), which means literally the beam that supports the roof. This symbol makes sense when you consider the importance of the various 'Trees of Life', connecting heaven and earth and providing access to the upper and lower world. Such world-trees can be found in plenty of Eurasian 'shamanic' systems and religions. Chinese cosmology is no exception to this belief. Over the centuries the tree was transformed into a pillar, and the world assumed the shape of a building, but the importance of the cosmic axis remained the same. The T'ai Chi is the 'Supreme Ultimate' as it supports the order and harmony of the world. This harmony is not static but depends on the subtle interplay of yin and yang. Indeed, yin and yang are only conceivable in relation with each other, and depending on the point of view.

In the *I Ching* these two energetic states are represented by two simple signs. Yin is shown as an open line ⚋ , while yang is drawn as a continuous line ⚊. These two signs form a binary system such as every mystic encounters in computers. It is one of those jokes that the famous philosopher/mathematician G. W. Leibniz (1646 - 1716) who invented the binary system, was influenced by the *I Ching* (see Hellmut Wilhelm). The story goes that Leibniz was struggling with binary mathematics, but didn't get anywhere, as he was trying to use a system based on the numbers one and two. A friend of his, Father Joachin Bouvet, who was a Jesuit on mission in Peking, sent him one of those *I Ching* charts showing the 64 signs arranged in a circle, but could not explain much about the diagram. Leibniz supposedly spent a lot of time staring at this image, trying to work out the method behind the arrangement. At some point he came upon the idea of basing his binary system on the numbers zero and one, which produced a lot of amazing maths and an entire generation happily at home in a box with a flickering screen. The chart was based on the so called Fu Hsi arrangement. Leibniz took the yang lines for zero and the yin lines for one and was surprised to find that the *I-Ching* showed the binary code for the numbers 0 - 63.

Out of the yin yang ingredients of the T'ai Chi the ten-thousand things developed, as you will know if you work with a computer. After being around for a while, however, these return into the simple yin yang polarity, and then this phenomenon dissolves into the Hun Tun once more. Translated into modern language, this simply means that computers are only useful as long as you know where and when to find the off switch. The same goes for consciousness and the myth of the individual personality, but you don't have to know this just to have fun with divination.

Nowadays most people associate the yin yang idea with the T'ai Chi symbol, i.e. the circle containing two tear shaped forms, one in black, the other in white, each of them containing a circle in the opposite colour:

The T'ai Chi itself is the empty circle and the drops represent the motion and interplay of yin and yang. Even for the superficial

Nü Kua

observer, it must be obvious that this signifies that yin contains yang and vice versa. Apparently this symbol became popular around the sixth century of our era. Much older is a Hun Tun symbol showing a circle containing a spiralling vortex in black and white, which had a similar meaning but a lot more dynamic energy.

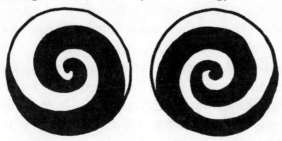

Duality

In this place it may be appropriate to say a few words about polarity. In Western philosophy, especially in the schools influenced by church dogmas, dualities are commonly assumed to be antagonistic. For centuries, people have believed in the conflict of heaven and hell, good fought against evil, life against death, god against the devil, soul against the flesh, and men and women were considered almost separate species. In Far Eastern philosophies, and in the Pagan religions of ancient Europe, polarities generally complement and support each other. The interaction of yin and yang was not seen as a struggle or conflict, but as a dance of changes involving frequent transformations.

What appears as yin today may seem to be yang tomorrow. In fact, Western thought - especially the New Age variety - is mistaken if it takes the two terms to mean things. There are plenty of authors who claim that yin is dark, cold, weak, passive and female. In real life, however, darkness can be warm; cold a very active force transforming the environment, and if the only women those writers know are weak, passive and cold one can only pity them. Likewise, if yang is strong, creative, bright, hard and active, the gods then help those poor males who try to live up to this image. What such lists reveal, first of all, is the errors one can make when one symbolizes abstract ideas with concepts and things, and mistakes the forms for what they were meant to suggest. What the early diviners had in mind was a lot less restrictive. Their aim was not definition but suggestion. When they used things to symbolize abstracts they did not mean that the abstracts are exactly like those things. Usually, things are too complicated and come tied in a web of conditions and beliefs which have nothing to do with the abstracts they were meant to represent.

A lot of Taoists did not believe in the reality of things at all. A well known adage states: 'whatever has form is not real' - as the forms you perceive are representations which you produce in your mind. Consequently, you would do well to treat the traditional symbols with a lot of caution. An enormous amount of rigid yin-yang cosmology was produced during the Ch'in and Han dynasties (from the third century BCE to 220 CE). During this period, philosophers tried to do their best to divide all phenomena of the world into the simple duality of yin and yang, which had a rather suffocating effect on society. The more items one tries to force into a symbol, the less meaning it has. It gets worse when one expects people to live up to such dogmas. The result of this interpretation was a sexist philosophy that bound women and men to certain forms of conduct and effectively stopped the development of scientific research.

Our early diviners had much simpler, but also more subtle interpretations in mind. The primal meaning of the shady and the sunny side was only slightly expanded. The *Shih-Ching* (8th Century BCE) simply remarks that yin refers to cold and dark weather, the overcast sky and dark and cool storage rooms, while yang is described as sunny and warm. Even these simple terms are just metaphors.

First Exercise - Yin and Yang

For those who want to develop an intimate understanding of the *I Ching*, it would be useful to pause now and to do a little practical exercise.

Sit or lie comfortably and calm down. Allow yourself to go into a pleasant and relaxed trance state, using whatever method you like. A typical Taoist technique is to observe the breathing. This does not mean effort, control or interference. It is miles away from the notion of breath-control as taught by some schools of Yoga.

Simply allow your attention to dwell on the motion of your belly as your breath flows. A general awareness of the belly is quite enough. It doesn't have to be a precise spot nor should there be any intent in the motion. Breathing is a very subtle meditation. For many people its very simplicity may be the greatest obstacle. Forget about technique, about purpose or the task of doing it 'properly'. Breath flows on its own accord. As you observe, it becomes gentle, calm and refined, and so does your awareness. Allow your breath to become soft. From time to time your attention may wander elsewhere, or you may forget what you are doing. This is fine. Enjoy it.

Close your eyes and imagine an open yin line   - -

You would do well to make this image interesting. A diffuse representation of a distant and small line, for example, is not too stimulating. It may become more exciting when you make it bigger, bring it closer, add colour, glow and some brightness. Make it shine, glitter and gleam, if you like. Look at it from above, eye level and below. Make it three dimensional if you like and let it pulse with vitality. These are just a few things you can do with your mind to turn on your imagination. Some of them may work, and increase your emotional response, others may not, as your mind is unique and has its own peculiar ways of making images interesting. Find out which forms of representation turn you on and use them. The idea is to make the image as stimulating as possible.

Next, develop some fantasies that suit the yin symbol. You could start out with the concept of 'the shady side' (of a mountain) and imagine what it is like there. Maybe you already have some memories that are suitable for this. Or you could go for a walk in your imagination and explore a dream mountain. In early Chinese thought, mountains were sacred places in touch with heaven. There is much to be learned when you dare to dream. Use the same methods as before to make this vision an interesting one. For most people, a large and colourful vision is a lot more impressive than a tiny picture in the distance.

Make the representation as vivid as you can. If you like to, include the other senses. Feel the coolness and the moist air, hear the birds and the insects, if any, and go exploring in your mind. If your inner voice accompanies the vision, use a soft and gentle modulation, and speak slow and calm if you like. From time to time you can superimpose the image of the yin line over the scenery and the events to associate the vision and the symbol.

This is your chance to be creative. You shouldn't confine your imagination to the shady mountainside but allow it to roam to other phenomena which could represent yin to you. These might be an overcast sky, a fresh wind, dark clouds, falling rain, flowing waters, a serene moon or the coming of night-time, plus whatever else you associate with passive, calming, stabilizing energy. Connect these images with the yin sign which will soon become a storehouse of related visions. End your visions by telling yourself that all the phenomena you witnessed are related in some way to the idea of yin.

Then pause a while, and go through the same process with the yang line ▬, the sunny side, the warm season and whatever seems related. It may be useful to accompany the yang visions by dynamic moods. Make your inner voice sound strong, fast and excited. Keep your body relaxed and your breath smooth, and enjoy calling and receiving.

Just what you specifically imagine is your own business. It might be a glaring sun, a flash of lightning, the eruption of a volcano, if you enjoy dramatic images; or the bursting of buds, the migrations of beasts, or the wind driving clouds over the sky, if you delight in more subtle images. It doesn't have to be specifically Chinese, nor need it fit the concepts of the classical writers. The important thing is that it suits you.

If you want to make a thorough job of this trance adventure, repeat it a couple of times before you proceed with the next step. The better you prepare, the easier will your development be.

Fu Hsi and Nü Kua

In Chinese prehistory, two primal beings represented the forces of yin and yang. These were Lady Nü Kua and Lord Fu Hsi, who was also known as Taihao, the great brightness. The two lived at the very beginning of time when the directions of space were still mingled, the round tent of heaven did not entirely cover the square wagon of earth, fire and water had not been divided and everything became everything else.

Fu Hsi and Nü Kua

Fu Hsi (Fuxi) and Nü Kua (Nüwa) lived at the mountain of heaven. Both had dragon shape and long twisted tails, as you can see in the illustration. They were brother and sister, but in spite of this they invented marriage and its rituals. This is called learning by doing.

The two appear prominently as inventors. Nü Kua had the skill of melting metals and other substances. Once, the monster Gonggong, who had the head of a human with flaming red hair but the body of a serpent (a comet?) tried to destroy the earth. When its plans failed, it had a fit of rage and smashed the northern pillar of the earth. The heavy impact made the silken canopy of heaven tilt dangerously. A devastating flood rushed over the earth, but Nü Kua banished it and melted metals and precious stones to repair the pillar. Then she stabilized the four directions of space, patched up the tent of heaven and stilled the rushing waters with a barrier of reeds and ashes. She created humans out of clay and burned them in her oven.

Fu Hsi, who occasionally wore the head of a bull with the snout of a tiger, is famed for inventing fishing and hunting, and for taming the hundred animals. He is also the inventor of cooked meals, and of simple string instruments. His sign is the set angle while hers is the compass of heaven. At this point you might observe that it is by no means easy to work out who of the two represents the force of yin or yang. Don't worry. As both of them were competent shapeshifters it only occasionally happened that they assumed a sexual form and coupled.

The eight signs, or Pa Kua, were an invention of Fu Hsi.

When in early antiquity Pao Hsi (Fu Hsi) ruled the world, he looked upward and contemplated the images in the heavens; he looked downward and contemplated the patterns on earth. He contemplated the markings of birds and beasts and the adaptations to the regions. He proceeded directly from himself and indirectly from objects. Thus he invented the eight trigrams in order to enter into connection with the virtues of the light of the gods and to regulate the conditions of all beings.

Ta Chuan, Wilhelm translation

When you take the continuous and the open lines that represent yang and yin and combine them in groups of three, you get eight possible combinations. These are the eight trigrams from which the 64 hexagrams of the *I Ching* were developed.

The Three Levels

For the start it may be useful to learn about the eight trigrams. Each of them is made up of three lines which are usually drawn starting at the bottom. I would like to propose that we are dealing with three levels. This is a bit on the speculative side but it does make sense when applied to the symbolism of the trigrams. Each level has a yin or yang line to show its energetic state. The symbology of the three levels is one of the most ancient models of the world. It is not specifically Chinese but can be found in dozens of cultures.

You can find parallels to this structure in the beliefs of numerous Central Asian cultures, among the shamans of Siberia and even in the myths of ancient Europe. It is in the Far East, however, that the model of the three planes was most widely used. The basic idea is this. The world, as far as we can know it, consists of three levels.

The Deep

At the bottom is the level of the earth and the underworlds beneath the surface. It is the realm of manifest form, of soil, ground, stone and enduring matter, the source of crystals and metal and the hidden space through which the deep waters flow. In the earth level the trees and plants have their roots and find their nourishment. As scenery, the earth level shapes the environments where living beings move and dwell. Closely aligned is the land of the ancestors, who have their graves in the earth, and hence, the idea of the past. The ancestors are not only human beings and past selves but also the entire range of life forms that exist in the genetic inheritance of our cells. This connects the earth level with the strong instincts, passions, urges and survival drives. In the human being, the earth level can be symbolized by the legs, genitals and belly.

The Middle

The middle range is the world of humans, or, more generally, the world we share with other lifeforms. Here we live and move in the living biosphere. Plants grow and blossom in this plane, beasts search for food and mates, and humans build houses and cities to manifest their dream of life. This is the social realm, the world of personality and society, and it is characterized by interaction and communication. It is also the most transitory and deceptive level. To function in their self-made world, humans organize their groups with laws and customs. They establish beliefs and traditions, they learn trades and professions, they assume masks and identify with them. The result of this process is the personality, the concept of an 'I' that has independent existence and divides the world into good and bad, true and false, mine and yours. In the middle realm you can find such forces as reason and emotion, both of which depend on the ego. In the human being, the middle level may be symbolized with the upper belly, the breast, shoulders, arms and hands.

The Height

The upper level is symbolized by heaven. Here you can find the great creative and destructive forces that determine the seasons and the time of day. Heaven is the passage of sun and moon, the planets and the stars. It is the frequent change of weather, the source of day and night, of rain and drought, of thunder and mist. As the land of the gods, people looked up into the height and sacrificed to gain the favour of the celestial ones. Chinese cosmology considers heaven the perfect and ideal domain. In heaven, you can observe both the enduring and predictable motions of the stars and the planets but also the activity of forces that have no form but nevertheless exert their influence. The upper level represents the divine energies, the land from which enlightenment and inspiration come. This is the realm of the immortals, that is, the native home of those who have transcended ego and become timeless and unlimited. In the human being, heaven is the head and the empty space above.

These three levels are central to many Eastern philosophies. You can find them in the meditations of practical Taoism, where they are visualized into the human body. The deep level of earth and the underworlds is located in the alchemical oven of the belly, between navel and genitals. The middle range, peopled by humans and beasts and vegetation, is visualized in the breast, while the heavenly realm is in the head. Each of these levels might be imagined as a vessel, a hollow, a cavity, a field, an aperture or an oven, containing a characteristic vapour in a specific colour and an important spirit (see Saso 1978). In these rituals of union with the Tao, the vapours are circulated within body, and the three spirits are visualized.

Do you remember how the Hun Tun gave birth to yin and yang, and how the two generated the ten-thousand things? The pattern of creation can be reversed and mind can become no-mind and return to the beginning. In the rite of exteriorizing the spirits, the Taoist visualizes the spirits as they dwell in the body. Then they are projected outwards. Spirit after spirit is released out of its microcosmic dwelling place and into the temple space. At the same time, the spirits are simplified. The spirits of the ten-thousand things blend to become the five energies. The five 'movers' simplify into the three spirits of the planes. These return into yin and yang, which in turn becomes the primal simplicity of the Hun Tun. In this state, which is no state, the Taoist has become entirely formless and void. Beyond it, the nameless, original Tao might be realized, if only there were someone left to realize it.

This is one of the most admirable parts of Taoist ritual. The meditative ritual reverses the order of creation as the Taoist returns to the beginning. The process, described more fully by Michael Saso, is called Hsin-Chai, or '*fasting (voiding) the heart*'. As the rite proceeds, the ritualist becomes increasingly empty, and union with the nameless, inconceivable Tao occurs naturally when the Taoist is absent and has even forgotten the purpose of the ritual. Mind you, after the meditation the spirits are allowed to come back into the body again.

The full ritual is a somewhat complicated process that can take years to develop. Much of it, especially in regard to the proper visualizations of the spirits and their appearance, is shrouded in obscure symbolism or taught by oral instruction. Many of the terms used to describe the ritual are misleading. The 'heart', for example, can be a word meaning attention, but it can also refer to other phenomena, depending on context and level of understanding.

What colours are visualized, and what spirits are exteriorized is a complicated question you needn't be bothered by. There are countless schools of Taoism, many of them happily involved in small-scale warfare with each other, and of course each school has the proper attributions and knows the true associations, while the rival sects are ritually cursed for their false and misleading teachings. In these matters, ritual Taoism is regrettably much like the countless orders and cults in Western magic and witchcraft.

If you want to know about the specific spirits that correspond to the three levels, a couple of Chinese names won't help you much. But consider the function! The three are in charge of primordial breath (original consciousness), life-giving Ch'i energy, and the essence of physical vitality, seen from top to bottom and beginning to manifestation. Ask your own spirits who is in charge of these functions in your own system and learn from them. You can learn a lot about the three planes when you study and enjoy the art of China, Korea and Japan. In each painting, statue or flower arrangement, the three levels and their meaning are the guiding principle. But let us return to the eight signs.

Exercise Two: the three planes

In each of the three levels, a yin or yang line is drawn. Before we come to consider their effect, you would do well to meditate on them.

Have a pause now, relax, close your eyes, and imagine that you travel through the three levels of the world, and through their counterparts in your body. Observe what happens on each plane. The more vividly you imagine this, the easier will your understanding of the trigrams evolve. You could start by imagining all sorts of events that are associated with the deep realm and the underworld. As you persist, more and more ideas will associate themselves, and before long the deep realm will become a real place and consciousness for you. Then experience the middle world and finally gather a lot of fitting images and visions suited to the higher realm of heaven and the upperworlds. If you do this imagination exercise a few times you will find that the three levels come to life for you. The imagination will become stable and you will find access with greater ease.

Heaven and earth have a beginning. Heaven is invisible and creates, earth is visible and forms. Union and harmony of heaven and earth are the great way to all conception. (. . .)

When entities unite they conceive, when they separate, birth occurs.
Who understands union knows the law of conception and heaven and earth are in balance.
In this state of harmony all accords with its own nature and shows its original form.
From the Spring and Autumn Annals of Lü Bu We c. 240 BCE

By now we have almost all material available to practise *I Ching* divination with minimum equipment. I hope that you have done the visualization, as otherwise, little of what follows will make sense to you. What you have developed so far is a number of associations with yin and yang and a model of the world that has three levels. We shall now bring these two items together and find out what happens. This means that you'll have to memorize the eight signs, quite a simple task, considering that some professional diviners of antiquity memorized the whole set of 64 signs plus variations and commentaries. As you will see later on this is not necessary, unless you want to, as the eight signs are sufficient to let the visions come.

We will start out with the two simplest signs as you already know much about them.

This is the trigram CHIEN (Quian) and the sign of heaven. As you can see all three levels are totally yang. Chien shines and radiates, it creates, expands and overwhelms with its unlimited energy. Chien is pure activity unhindered by matter. Imagine that all you visualized regarding the yang sign is happening on all three levels at once, and go beyond it. The result is impressive, but you wouldn't want to live there. All levels are active on full power. Through its sheer strength, Chien is unstable. As a consciousness state, it may produce amazing effects, but is in danger of burning itself out.

Chinese literature associates Chien with the following concepts:

Heaven, the creative, sovereignty, fighting, strength, height, and adds the following (which may or may not make sense to you): head, horse, round (like heaven), metal, coldness, ice, deep red, tree fruit, early winter, jade. In the family structure, which is one of the essentials of Chinese thought, Chien is symbolized by the father. In the magical system of Tso Tao, the Tao of the left, it has the title K'ai, the opening. It represents the head of the serpent and is used for magical attacks by those who have nothing better to do.

is the sign KUN, called earth and the receptive. This kua (divinatory sign) is the absolute opposite of Chien as regards the energy level, but shows some similarity in the fact that it is quite as extreme. To find out about Kun you should imagine a world in which all three levels are totally yin. Where Chien shows an excess of the constellating force (shen) which induces change and active development, Kun represents an excess of the structural force (ling) which fixes, manifests and materializes. The sign tends to be massive, solid and inert. There is a heavy quality to it, which is full of latent potential, and ready to take on any form. As a consciousness state, Kun comes close to dreamless sleep. However, these comments are just examples. Much more interesting is the question what the sign means to you. Do the visualization and find out.

In literature the following suggestions are given: Earth, the receptive, protection, nourishing, useful, deep, yielding, as well as: cattle, the belly, cauldron, cloth, the plains, wealth, form, the wagon (the earth was believed to be a square wagon under a round tent), black earth, rest and early autumn. In the family, Kun was represented as the mother. Tso Tao calls it Szu, or death.

From these two signs, the other six were generated. An old myth claims that originally, heaven and earth were in continuous union with each other. After a while, they conceived and gave birth to children. These, however, had no space to live. When they became strong enough, they forced heaven and earth apart and populated the middle world. All children are of a mixed nature. Originally, they may have been forces of nature, but there is more to them than that. Keep in mind that Chinese cosmology is not so much concerned with things as with abstract energies, sentiences, and their transformation. The things are only there to represent more subtle influences. There are, for instance, two systems of attributing the following signs to the family structure. The first proposes that all kua with only one yin line are daughters and that all kua with only a single yang line are the sons. The other claims that those signs who have a yin bottom line are daughters and the ones with a yang bottom are sons. Consequently, it is not very easy to decide if some trigrams happen to be sons or daughters, or both. If you take these symbols to refer to real people you may arrive at the insight that prehistoric China saw a lot of sex changing. This, of course, is not the purpose of comparing the kua with a family. What the Taoists had in mind is a genealogy, an order of development.

Exercise Three: The eight signs

To make the most of my explanations, I suggest that you experience each of the eight signs in vision. After reading about the sign, you can make yourself comfortable, relax and close your eyes. Observe your breath as it flows, calm your inner voice, slow down leisurely and focus on the sign. As in the exercises you did before, you can visualize the abstract form of the lines. Make it impressive! Connect this image with whatever seems appropriate. With the sign Li for instance, you could imagine all sorts of fires and fire customs that come into your mind. You might also remember fires you have seen, and invent fires you would like to see, plus all sorts of phenomena which may seem related to the fire idea, such as the sun, the stars, lightning, the molten core of our planet, fireworks and the human emotions and activities which partake, in your opinion, of a fiery nature. The more you associate with the sign, the easier will your divination be. Invent several visions for each sign, and keep associating them with the abstract form of the lines.

This is the sign LI which is known by such symbols as fire, the sun and the clinging. There is of course a great deal that might be said about the meaning of fire in any society. Fire is one of the essentials of life, and has been from the early stone ages, when five or six hundred-thousand years ago, the 'Peking Man' had fire pits, which were carefully guarded for generations. The first fire was born out of the union of heaven and earth in the shape of the lightning flash. Long before people learned how to make fire, they knew how to find and nourish it. As a source of light and heat, fire allowed our early semi-human ancestors, and also our own species, to survive the various ice ages. Such remarks may seem unnecessary. I make them to remind you of the essential importance of simple things. Modern folk, with central heating and electric ovens tend to forget what fire used to mean in earlier times.

If you care to remember and understand, relax, close your eyes, and allow your mind to think of fire for a while.

Let us take a look at the abstract sign now. Li has a strong heaven and a strong earth. The middle range, i.e. the human world, is of yin nature, and therefore more passive and receptive. If we apply this vision to the human being, we might encounter a consciousness with strong inspiration (heaven) and strong instincts (earth). The human being, the ego, is receptive, and channels the vital energies coming from above and below. This is the condition of genius, in which the gods and the beasts enjoy full freedom of expression while the human personality withdraws and allows everything to happen. The early commentators of the *I Ching* represented Li with such concepts as fire, sun, the clinging, warmth, light, brilliance and lightning. They also associated the pheasant, the phoenix, eyes, armour (the sign is hard on the outside and soft in the centre), helmet, tortoise, shells and snails, weapons, drought and summertime. Tso Tao calls it Ching, or vantage point.

is the sign KAN which has several meanings. First of all Kan is called the abysmal, and is symbolized by water in its dangerous form. Kan can be the great ocean, or a threatening flood. It can be a roaring stream, a deluding fog or a devastating rainstorm. It can even signify the greatest abyss of them all, the stellar void of the beginning. The image offers several insights. The central line, representing the human world, is active and busy between a passive height and depth. This could be a picture of a tiny boat floating on the waters of infinity, a space ship travelling through the great black void, or a person walking over a bridge across a bottomless chasm. As a consciousness, Kan represents the poor, limited ego all on its own, without the support of the divine (heaven) and the wisdom of the instincts (earth). This can mean doubt, crisis, fear and dissolution of belief and personality. In Chinese thought, a crisis is not necessarily something bad. Crisis contains danger, but it also offers great chances. Where the personality comes apart, it also has the chance to reform in a better shape. Literature associates Kan with water, danger, the ocean, rain, dampness, the abysmal, clouds and fog. Other attributions are pig and boar, ears, ditches, ambush, curves, bows, the moon, blood-red and black colour, thieves, spies, stumbling and wintertime. Tso Tao calls it hsiu, or rest.

Here is the sign SUN, called the gentle, penetrating, and symbolized by wind and wood. Sun is a subtle energy. It has a strong heaven and strong humanity, making it mobile and changeful. Its earth level is passive or latent, however, and so Sun is always on the move, shapeless, formless, and yet all present. The wind may be invisible, but it surrounds the world and penetrates every-where. The air we breathe comes from the breath cycles of the trees, plants and algae, and maybe the ancient Taoists knew of this fact when they claimed that wind is born in the forest. As consciousness, the sign Sun may reflect a mobile nature that is full of inspiration (heaven) and social interaction, thought and talk (human level). What is momentarily absent is its grounding in flesh, the desires, hungers, lusts and drives of the bestial part of our being. Sun is like the wide sky and the swift passage of the wind as it flows through the branches. It is a useful state to learn or discuss philosophy, provided one does not forget to eat once in a while. Literature associates Sun with air, wind, breath, wood, gentleness, penetration, dissolution, distribution and the undifferentiated. Other symbols are the cockerel, hips, work and motion, length, height, white colour, breeze, storm and early summer. Tso Tao calls it Tu, or blockade.

is the sign CHEN (Zhen), called the arousing or thunder. This is a very passionate event. Chen, while related to fire, portrays the dangerous and overwhelming side of the element. You could visualize a great thunderstorm building up and releasing its fury in hail, lightning, thunder and rain. You could imagine earthquakes, and erupting volcanoes releasing the fire of the deep. Or think of the great force of the arousing as it pumps millions of tons of sap through the forest trees in spring, bursting buds, unfolding leaves, and sending the light-hungry shoots of new plants through the hard soil and into the open air. And what of your own hormone production? Applied to the microcosmos, Chen shows a consciousness in which the divine and the human levels are open and receptive, while the deep realm of flesh and lust and instinct gives an irresistible impulse. The sign has its emphasis on the genitals, as you probably noticed straightaway, and these are all set to go out and have fun. There is also a lot of mythology related to thunder. The commentaries describe Chen with the metaphors thunder, arousing, motion, beginning, vehemence, strong growth, and add dragons, a foot, outfolding, the great road, reeds, green bamboo, buds, shoots, dark yellow and springtime. Tso Tao names it Shang, or injury.

is called KEN (Gen), keeping still, resting, and is symbolized by a mountain. You can see that Ken has an active heaven while the human and earthly levels lie receptive and latent. In nature, this is symbolized by the mountain, which is, remains, lasts and endures. Mountains were believed to be the homes of gods and spirits. Ancient China had a thriving mountain cult with numerous sacred heights which were visited by the faithful for the rituals of pilgrimage, prayer and sacrifice. Even the regents derived their right to rule from having visited sacred mountains, and were considered as the representatives of the divine forces that found their gate to earth on the summits. Occasionally the sign was referred to as 'the gate of life' or 'the gate of hell' depending on the mood of the mountain. People rarely lived on mountains (except for hermits and visionaries) as these are not usually favourable for settlements. High mountains offer a grandiose scenery, but they are also sites of hard weather and scant shelter. Some ascetics made do with caves, and caves are also suggested by the sign, which is hard at the top but has a wide opening in its middle and bottom layers. In general, the strong line at the top shows the influence of heaven, absolute and eternal. The human level is latent, showing that society and its rules are suspended on the height, and so is the earth level, indicating that the fields and settlements are far below. As a consciousness, Ken may suggest a person in trance who has forgotten body and identity, and has dissolved into the timeless and ideal realm of heavenly harmony. Ken is called mountain, standing still, rest, peace, silence, completion. Other attributes are dog, the hand (and the ability to hold firmly), rocks, stone, mountain paths, gates, doors, orifices, fruit, seeds, grain, rats, guardians (eunuchs), watchmen, and early springtime. Tso Tao calls it Sheng, or life.

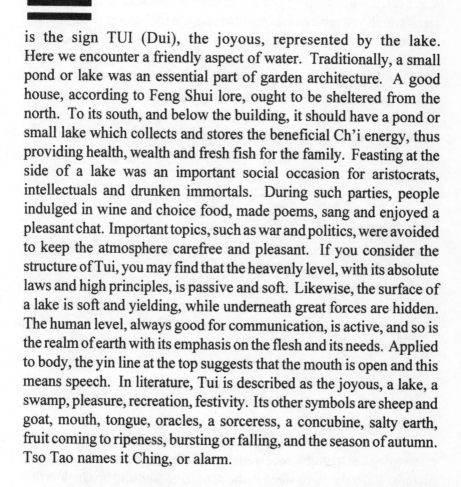

is the sign TUI (Dui), the joyous, represented by the lake. Here we encounter a friendly aspect of water. Traditionally, a small pond or lake was an essential part of garden architecture. A good house, according to Feng Shui lore, ought to be sheltered from the north. To its south, and below the building, it should have a pond or small lake which collects and stores the beneficial Ch'i energy, thus providing health, wealth and fresh fish for the family. Feasting at the side of a lake was an important social occasion for aristocrats, intellectuals and drunken immortals. During such parties, people indulged in wine and choice food, made poems, sang and enjoyed a pleasant chat. Important topics, such as war and politics, were avoided to keep the atmosphere carefree and pleasant. If you consider the structure of Tui, you may find that the heavenly level, with its absolute laws and high principles, is passive and soft. Likewise, the surface of a lake is soft and yielding, while underneath great forces are hidden. The human level, always good for communication, is active, and so is the realm of earth with its emphasis on the flesh and its needs. Applied to body, the yin line at the top suggests that the mouth is open and this means speech. In literature, Tui is described as the joyous, a lake, a swamp, pleasure, recreation, festivity. Its other symbols are sheep and goat, mouth, tongue, oracles, a sorceress, a concubine, salty earth, fruit coming to ripeness, bursting or falling, and the season of autumn. Tso Tao names it Ching, or alarm.

If you have done the visualization exercises for each sign, some of these images will make sense to you. Maybe you have also received other insights, and this is an excellent sign that the Pa Kua are coming to life in your mind. The earliest diviners of ancient China had no books of commentaries to look things up. They had some teachings transmitted by oral tradition, memorized in all likelihood in rhyme and their own subjective insights that made the eight signs such an excellent system of inspiration. Consider that if you ask your deep mind (or the gods, spirits, intelligences if you like) a question, the signs which you receive are meant to suggest the answer. Lazy people may look this answer up in a book, where they will find the accumulated insights of a lot of other people. While these may occasionally be of use, there are many ways in which you differ from those authors, and where a really good answer can only come from your own self. As the deep mind supplies the sign, it has an interest in telling you something useful. Maybe you'll find it in a book, but certainly you can find it in your own visions. The signs are not the answer. The answer is suggested by the signs.

Classical Divination

The sorcerers of ancient China used several methods to divine the unknown. One method that is occasionally mentioned in popular literature (I forgot where) was to carve the eight kua into the shell of a tortoise. After appropriate ceremonies, the shell was put into a ritual fire, where it remained until it cracked. After the rite, the fire was extinguished and the shell examined. Usually, the cracks touched one or more trigram, and these were interpreted to provide an answer.

I have no idea if there is any archaeological evidence for this method. Tortoise shells with the eight kua, as we know them, have not been found.

What can be found, however, are fairly recent illustrations of the numerological pattern received by Yü the Great. Usually these pictures show the eight signs in the pattern of dark and bright dots that Yü the Great saw on the back of the tortoise shell in his famous vision. Again, there are no such tortoise shells among the oracular items of early China. The pictures show a popular arrangement, but this pattern does not appear on the items unearthed by the archaeologists.

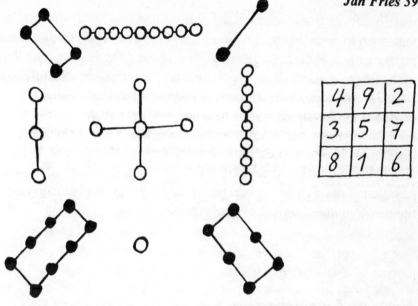

The pattern on the tortoise shell as recieved by Yü the Great

Nevertheless tortoise shells and shoulder bones were highly popular for divination. Such shells often show a complicated arrangement of drilled holes making it easier for the fire to crack them. It has been hypothesized that cracks on the outer surface of the tortoise shell refer to yang while those on the inner to yin, but as it is there is not enough evidence to be sure of anything. Plenty of tortoise shells, dating from the 13th century BCE have been dug up in recent excavations of the capitol of the Shang dynasty in Henan. These differ from the pictures of later periods. Where the illustrations show the pattern of Yü on the back of the tortoise shells, the ancient oracle used the belly plate of the reptile. The shells show inscriptions and have been employed for oracular purposes. It has been proposed that holes were drilled into the shells and that a red hot metal rod was pressed into the holes. This made cracks appear on the other side, and these yielded an answer to the question. How the interpretation was found and why the questions and answers were noted on the shells remains a tricky issue.

Recent excavations in China have brought to light a wealth of lots, usually carved from tortoise shell or bone and inscribed with oracles that seem to resemble the *I Ching*. These systems of divination are a lot more obscure than the classical way of using the *I Ching*. The lots of the Shang dynasty show a specific oracular script (see examples on page 71) but none of the trigrams you are now familiar with. The first evidence for the trigrams with open and continuous lines comes from the Chou dynasty that overthrew the Shang and reformed religion by installing 365 new deities, most of them deceased heroes and immortals. In between these forms exist a form of divination that had tri- and hexagrams (as well as the odd penta- and heptagram) but expressed them with numerological symbols instead of lines.

The sixty-four signs

One day, my Wu Shu teacher Kim Da Ga Nee amazed me with an account of diviners he had seen in some countries of South-East Asia. Usually these people simply set up a humble stand of wood, paper and cloth, out on the street, so their clients could have a bit of oracular advice while going about their business. Generally, these diviners did not bother to consult books, nor did they count stalks or work the three coins. Usually they were not even concerned about the changing lines that the Duke of Chou interpreted in such detail. What they did was simple and direct. They shook a single coin in their hands, and concentrated on the client's question. Then they slammed the coin on the table (apparently the noise is part of the ritual) and looked whether the yin or the yang side was on top. This produced the bottom line, as the *I Ching* signs grow from bottom to the top. Two more throws and they had the first trigram, another three and the full hexagram, consisting of two trigrams, was complete. Each of the 64 hexagrams of the *I Ching* is composed of two trigrams, and if you know the trigrams, you can combine them and find out what sort of vision you have. Usually, they tend to be colourful, and often surprising.

The invention of the 64 hexagrams is ascribed to another legendary emperor of prehistory. This was the 'divine farmer' Shennong, who was also known as Yandi, fire-lord, the Red Emperor. Shennong invented agriculture and taught how the five grains can be cultivated. Like the other mythical emperors, he is not quite human by nature, and appears in Taoist rites as one of the great spirits who guard the circle. His body seems human enough but his head is that of a bull. He established the great feasts of harvest time and invented the plough, whose marks may remind you of the shape of the hexagrams. Yandi is also the god of medicine. He explored the effects of hundreds of plants by ingesting them. In the end one of them, the 'bowel breaking weed' (or the 'hundred legged vermin', as some say) proved too strong and killed him.

Exercise Four: One coin divination

To practise divination you only need one coin and the visualizations you built up so carefully. Nor does it have to be a coin. Quite as good is a cowrie shell (which has an open yin and a bulging yang side) or a smooth pebble with two different sides. Perhaps you would like a concave and a convex side for yin and yang, or prefer a different pattern that suggests the right ideas to you. To make the pebble work, you should identify the sides clearly.

Look at the yin side. Imagine the open line vividly, and project it into the pebble. Recall all the visions you had of the yin energy, and send them into the proper side of the pebble. Then turn the pebble around and identify its yang side with the yang line and with all your yang visions. Do this several times, so that each side is clearly associated. The next item you need is a good, and preferably simple question. With 'simple' I mean that the words should be succinct and easy to understand. You could enquire what situation you are experiencing, what may develop if you do something or what comments the *I Ching* has to offer regarding some specific topic. It's like consulting an expert. The oracle can give you an estimate of development and tendency. Deciding what to do remains your own business.

As you ask your question, shake the pebble in your cupped hands. Keep asking the question and shake rhythmically. Repetition gives your deep mind (or the spirits) a chance to focus properly on the topic, to choose an answer and prepare a vision. Give yourself time. After a while you will feel the impulse to cast your pebble. Do this six times and you have your answer. Say thank you for this gift. Now visualize the hexagram, i.e. the two trigrams on top of each other. Allow them to become meaningful. This is a creative process. Some answers may be easy to imagine, such as thunder over the earth, the wind over a lake, or rain over a mountain. Reversed, they are less common in nature, and may require creative invention to make sense. Thunder under the earth could mean an earthquake, if you like, or a shoot of grass working its way up through the soil. If you imagine the answer in its abstract form, say, as the arousing under the receptive, other images will come to mind. No doubt you can invent lots of meanings as you go along.

You will find that this ability becomes easier as you practise. Practise often, and not only with serious questions. Playing around with an ancient oracle may not seem respectful to serious-minded folk, but it certainly broadens the mind and produces experience, as well as good laughs. The spirits of the *I Ching* have a lot of humour when approached in a playful mood. If you only enquire about dead serious matters, they may laugh about you, and you wouldn't even notice. Indeed, taking divination too seriously is the best way to fool oneself. All an oracle can offer is educated guesses of the best informed parts of your mind. If you demand certainty from the *I Ching*, you will receive all the delusions that you deserve. A fascinating approach suggested by Kenneth Grant is to consult the oracle without asking a question. This permits the *I Ching* to comment on whatever matters at that moment, be it openly known or concealed. In fact, it can easily happen that the intelligences behind the oracle ignore your questions anyway and respond to whatever seems important to them.

If you have practised with this method for a while, you may have developed a number of fitting images that may represent the Pa Kua to yourself. These images will be quite subjective, and suit your personal world view. They are quite sufficient if you wish to practise divination or wish to create your own magical system to produce change in the world of appearances. On the other hand it could well be that you want to know more about the beliefs and customs that were associated in ancient China with the trigrams. This is useful for the full understanding of the Pa Kua. As J. Grinder emphasized, if you want to understand something, you should examine its function, structure *and* context. We have taken a close look at the structure of the signs, and their function for divination. The next section, before we consider their function for magick, is meant to give more insights into the cultural context, and the beliefs associated with those primal energies.

The primal energies

HEAVEN is the absolute realm from which everything originates. It is the abode of the Jade-Emperor, the regent of heaven, as well as the countless spirits and officials which constitute the heavenly hierarchy. Heaven, like the state, was believed to be a thriving bureaucracy. There were spirits in charge of various departments, these had underlings, and inferiors, plus officials which presided over certain dates of the 60 day cycle, liaison officers, speakers, ambassadors and whatnot. While this seemed neat and well organized to the serious-minded Confucians, there is plenty of Taoist literature satirizing heaven and its rulers for their inefficiency and dullness. Heaven was a moral institution. 'All under heaven' is an expression for the civilized world. What was not under the round canopy of heaven was the chaotic realm peopled by demons, barbarians, and vengeful spirits. The *Ch'ü Yüan* informs us that people suffering from need and exhaustion should call to heaven, as all good luck comes from above. People believed that heaven rewards good behaviour and punishes sins, and that the numbers of heaven determine the fate of individuals.

EARTH is the manifest aspect of the universe. Earth receives the creative impulse from heaven, and materializes it. Therefore the saying goes that earth has a hundred plans, while heaven has only one. Heaven is related with the general and earth with the particular, or as Lü Bu We has it '*the way of heaven is round, the way of the earth angular.*' When we come to earth we leave the realm of principle and become involved with conditions of event and other complications. Earth was believed to have a square shape, and this was reflected in the rectangular form of houses, villages, fields, city-walls and cemetaries. Its colour is yellow (the colour of the rich loess soil cultivated by the farmers) and its place is in the middle of the circle.

FIRE is associated with the south, the colour red and all bitter or burned tastes. Fire (Huo) sounds like life (Huo). On new year's day, people light fires for the god of wealth, a ritual meant to produce not only wealth but also a good life. On the 105th day after the winter solstice (around the 4th of April) all house fires are extinguished. This is known as the feast of cold food. The next day a new fire is made using the ancient method of the fire-drill, so that the fire may burn for another year. Walking on fire is a common practice on the 15th day of the first month.

WATER is found in the north of the circle, it is cold, black, and associated with wintertime. There is an immense amount of meaning to water, as it was used by Lao Tsu as a symbol for the Taoist and the subtle working of the Tao. Chapter 52 (8) (The figure outside the brackets refers to oldest Mawangdui version, that inside the brackets to standard version.) of the *Tao Te Ching* says that the highest goodness is like water. It benefits the ten-thousand things without striving, and it stays in the lowest place which all men loathe. Chapter 43 (78) adds that the weakest thing in the world, water, destroys the hardest stones and rocks. From such insights, water became one of the most complex metaphors in Chinese philosophy. The proverb '*Water moistens and moves down, fire flares and moves up*' ('*Hung Fan*') shows the relationship of Kan and Li. Just as Li could refer to the sun, Kan could be a reference to the moon, and to night. A considerable number of sexual metaphors involve the idea of water. Among the eight signs, water appears in two shapes, showing a pleasant (Tui) and a dangerous (Kan) face.

THUNDER is ruled by heaven. There is a special minister in charge of thunder, who has the task of finding and punishing evildoers. He manifests the wrath of heaven. Originally, he was a drummer riding a cart drawn by the dead. Later, he was portrayed as a red-haired beast with the head of a pig or a monkey, plus horns, claws, and leathery wings. '*Thunder is the sound of fire and the laughter of heaven*' (*Huang Ti Nei-Ching*). There are at least three schools of Taoist thunder magick, all of them based on the idea that the force of thunder can be assimilated by breathing, and stored in the gall bladder until required. Thunder magick was developed as an antidote against the Chia spirit sorceries of Tso Tao. Its main use is exorcism, but it can also be applied to bless, consecrate, or cure a cold. While thunder is said to control or break the enchantments of the Tao of the left, it is vulnerable when confronted with a number of taboo substances, such as urine, excrement and menstrual blood.

WOOD is related with the sign Sun, and the idea of wind. Its colour is blue-green, its season is spring and its direction the east. Wood may make you think of forests, and indeed, ancient China had plenty of large forests. People usually avoided them, as everyone knew there are dangerous ghosts, serpents, tigers and bandits in the greenwood. As the population grew, more land was cultivated, and the forests of antiquity shrank. Often enough it was only the sacred mountains where forests survived, and formed the holy groves where saints and immortals cultivated the Tao. In ancient times there were tree-cults for pine, spruce, ginko, willow, mulberry and several other species. It

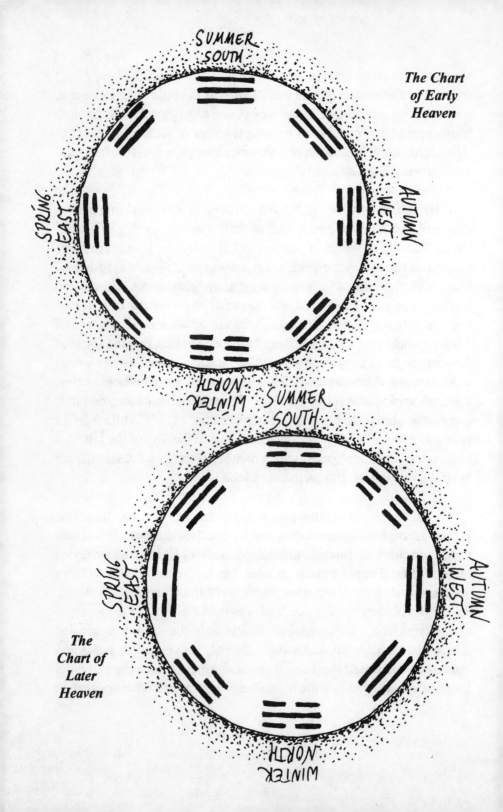

SUMMER
SOUTH

The Chart
of Early
Heaven

SPRING
EAST

AUTUMN
WEST

WINTER
NORTH

SUMMER
SOUTH

SPRING
EAST

AUTUMN
WEST

The
Chart of
Later
Heaven

WINTER
NORTH

seems that the religion of early China involved a number of ceremonies that took place in sacred groves. Chinese art shows many forest scenes, but usually the paintings include some civilizing elements, such as paths, pagodas or humble huts. The wild forest without human influence was not a popular topic.

WIND was symbolized by the god Feng Po in the Shang dynasty (until 1050 BCE) who manifests as a huge bird. This deity may be related to the great bird Peng who appears in Chuang Tsu's writings. Peng is so vast that it covers thousands of 'miles'. Its wings are like the clouds, it rises with the wind and it can stay in the air for up to six months. Wind is used for several metaphors. It can refer to speech and rumours, or to folk songs (as in the collection *Kuo-Feng, Wind of the Land*), but even more often to lovemaking. Waves of wind means making love, a person of wind and dust (the temporal world) is a courtesan. Also, a wind-mirror is a soothsayer, and wind (Feng) sounds like madness (Feng), which shows extensive experience with divination.

MOUNTAINS are among the oldest items in Chinese religion. There used to be a thriving mountain cult in early China, involving lots of sacred heights dedicated to various deities.

At first, the mountains represented the influence of heaven on earth. The K'un Lun mountain range in the west of China was considered the original mountain of heaven, where Fu Hsi and Nü Kua lived and the ten-thousand things had their beginning. These mountains had nine levels, which correspond to the nine heavens, as well as hanging gardens, sacred groves and wells containing the waters of immortality. For at least two-thousand years myths claim that the goddess of the west, Hsi Wang Mu, reigns on K'un Lun or in a cave within the mountain. There are signs that early China had the belief that several deities rule each mountain. In the north, the heights were seen as the places where the ancestors dwell, and occasionally young maidens were ritually married to mountains. To this day the five sacred mountains are popular for pilgrimage, offerings and ritual. Each has its own sacred forest on the top, as well as countless shrines, temples and sacred images. Even the emperors derived their authority from mountains. The better ones made pilgrimages to the sacred heights, and even the so called 'first emperor' Ch'in Shi Huang Ti tried to ascend the T'ai Shan. As heaven did not approve of him, a mighty storm arose which scattered the procession and forced the rain-drenched tyrant to hurry downhill.

The eight signs and magick

Apart from divination, the eight signs can be useful for magick and meditation. Simple as they are, they provide a system of cosmology which goes a long way beyond fortune telling. You have probably seen the eight signs arranged in a circle. Look at the illustration. First of all, you may notice that in these diagrams, the direction south is at the top. This may seem unusual for Westerners, who tend to have maps with north at the top, but then we are dealing with Chinese cosmology and this requires us to look at the world from a Chinese point of view. There are at least two ways of drawing this circle of enchantment. The first is called the diagram of primal heaven, the Ho T'u, and is attributed to Fu Hsi. In the chart of primal heaven, the trigrams are balanced and come in pairs. Fire is opposite of water, heaven opposes earth, wind balances with thunder and mountain with the lake. If you look at the way the signs are built up, you will see how this works. The circle of primal heaven describes a balanced world of harmony and perfection. It belongs to the inner universe, to the deep mind and to a realm that is utterly timeless. Standing in the centre of this circle, the Taoist is balanced in-between all forces and extremes.

Fu Hsi is also responsible for a curious map that he received in a vision when he was meditating at the river Ho.

The Liubo Game

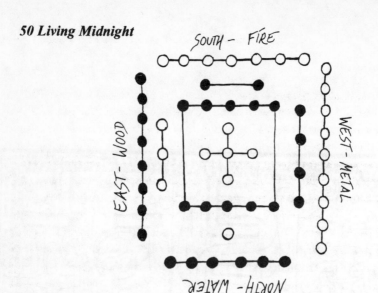

This diagram is called the map of the river Ho. It graced the flanks of a dragon-horse that rose from the waters to instruct the benevolent Green Emperor. The Ho T'u is an arrangement of black (yin) and white (yang) dots which describes the harmonic interplay of the numbers, the five moving powers and the directions of space. Its basic geometry follows the square shape of earth. The diagram is a complicated image of development. You can see that it has a ring of small numbers (1-5) and these are the creative forces. Around them are the larger numbers (6-10) which appear to manifest and complete the smaller numbers. In this system the energy of black water has the number one and is situated to the north. Fire has the number two and is in the south, its colour is red. Wood/wind is in the green direction of the east with the value of three and metal/precious stones comes from the white west with the number four. Earth in the centre corresponds with yellow and the number five. The other numbers are developed out of the former ones. This involves a great deal of highly refined numerology that we can do without for the time being.

This diagram is closely connected with the circle of earlier heaven and its condition of simplicity and primal perfection. It also reminds me of the square shape of the Chinese compass and of the ancient board game Liubo. This game was so popular that even the goddess Hsi Wang Mu, at that time a deity of death and the underworld, used to enjoy it in her otherworldly realm. Sadly the rules of this game (and oracle) have not survived. A number of Liubo boards have been excavated over the last years. They show a square layout and a number of chambers and passages, all of them decorated with gorgeous snakes, dragons and monstrosities. The square shape of the game-board connects it with the square shape of earth but also with the magical square of nine chambers that Yü the Great developed after his vision at the river Lo. We'll get to this story later on. To Fu Hsi the map of the river Ho represented the primal harmony of the beginning, the timeless realm of the first heavenly awareness. Its pattern can be explained to a degree, but its real purpose is to induce a certain consciousness. You can look into the map of the river Ho as if you would gaze into a mirror and observe the thoughts that are stimulated by its presence.

The primal heaven describes an almost perfect harmony. The Ho T'u can be understood as an image of the absolute and eternal. It is invoked to establish heavenly law on earth. Here on earth, things look somewhat differently, and another circle was developed.

This is the circle of the later heavens, the Lo Shu, attributed to Yü the Great, which shows how the trigrams appear on earth in the cycle of the seasons. Of the initial pairs, only the opposition of fire and water remains. The other signs are arranged according to the times of the year, the hours of the day and the directions. You find the Arousing in the east, where it refers to the first appearance of green plants in springtime. The Gentle, wind, nourishes the growth of the plants and is in the southeast. Fire is in the south, where it represents the heat of summer. Autumn begins with the Receptive in the southwest, while the Joyous, lake, represents the pleasures of fall in the west. The Creative, heaven, rules the northwest and the season of early winter, while dark, cold water rules the north and the season of midwinter. To the northeast lies the sign of the mountain, and of the gate of heaven and hell, this is the dark season between winter and spring. I shall not comment any further than this, as it will do you lots of good to work out the meaning of the heavenly charts.

You can often see circles of trigrams in Chinese art. There are several forms in which the trigrams can be arranged in a circle. One way, which I have chosen for this book, is to look at the signs from the inside of the circle. Occasionally one finds the same arrangement done from the outside point of view, in which case the circle looks somewhat different though it has the same meaning. Then there are several obscure arrangements which I have seen on Chinese talismans. Sometimes one encounters an odd arrangement on a photograph that has been printed the wrong way around. Some pictures of the circle of primal heaven switch the signs Kan and Li. This preserves the original balance, and is not really that important as the signs of this circle do not function in a series (as the Later Heaven circle does) but is a timeless balance. Last, there were at least two other arrangements of the trigrams in a circle shape that are suggested by the order of the signs in the Mawangdui version of the *I Ching*, we'll get to that matter later.

The two circles may remind you of the circles used by European and Oriental magicians. This is exactly the case. Most Westerners assume that Taoism is mainly a mystical activity involving contemplation, philosophy and a lot of doing without. While the works of Lao Tsu and Chuang Tsu have been translated into all European tongues, the practices of Taoism, involving a great deal of ritual and even more obscure meditations, have frequently been called 'superstitious perversions of the original, pure philosophy' and ignored by well meaning sinologists. This is quite a shame, as Tao without magick loses much of its charm.

Many of the Taoist rituals take place in a sacred space marked by the eight trigrams. Between them, the ritualist performs a dance that leads from sign to sign. This is the Yü Pu, the dance step of Yü.

The Dance of Yü

Would you like a little story? Once upon a time in distant prehistory, a great flood threatened the world. You may notice that Chinese myth has several great floods, and several mythical heroes and heroines were busy dealing with the raging waters.

In those distant days, the emperor Yao required a hero who would stop the flood. A certain Kun, son of the Black Emperor, volunteered for the job. Armed with mighty powers, Kun tried to fight the flood by building dykes and barriers. He did that for nine years without getting anywhere until Yao had had enough and gave the job to Shun. The loss of face was so hard to bear that Kun rebelled against the imperial order. To no avail. He was first banished from court and later executed. His spirit refused to die but became a restless ghost that haunts the wilderness in the shape of a bear or a fish.

Shun, who was famous for his love of justice, became emperor after Yao. He gave the task of stopping the flood to Kun's son, Yü, who had the head of a bird and the body of a bear. One day Yü the Great was walking along the side of the great stream Lo. The water was high and flecks of foam were dancing on the speeding waves. Yü stood at the shoreline, staring wide-eyed into the turbulence and glitter of the swirling waters. Before his eyes the mysterious pass opened. The mysterious pass can be anywhere. It can be in the flow of water, in the falling of raindrops, in the floating mists in the valley and in the dance of bright green leaves in the wind. It can be the song of the cicadas, the resting of a rock or the glitter of stars in the night-sky. When the mind becomes still, the mysterious pass opens.

Yü was blessed by heaven. Before his eyes a huge dark tortoise rose from the churning waves. On its shell, the tortoise had a strange pattern. It looked a bit like the map of the river Ho, but unlike it, the new pattern only had nine numbers and involved some diagonal symmetries. As Yü was staring at this amazing tortoise he realized that the pattern on its shell could be drawn as a square of nine chambers. Each chamber had a number and the sum of each line was fifteen. This square could be aligned with the circles of the eight trigrams. If you

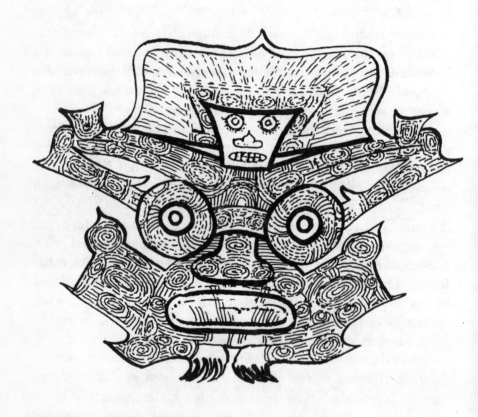

Zoomorphic entity on a gong (ritual vessel) c. 2800 BCE, Fanshaw, Yuhang, Zhejiang

imagine a circle of eight signs and place the square of the river Lo in its centre you get an order of events. You can move from trigram one to trigram two to trigram three and soon the motion becomes a dance.

Yü the great banished the flood by transforming fully into the form of a bear. In this shape, he danced between the eight kua until the waters withdrew and the world and its seasons returned to harmony.

The dance of Yü appears in literature from the second century BCE. It is frequently used in ceremonies of offering or exorcism. Dancing, however, is not the only activity of Yü in his fight with the flood. Still in the shape and awareness of a bear, he tore up the ground and dug deep channels so that the waters could flow off more easily. He scratched some signs into the earth and a dragon appeared who drove the waters away. In these strategies, Yü showed more wisdom than his father. Where Kun had tried to block the rush of the waters, Yü led them along controlled channels. He directed the path of the torrents and made them exhaust their violence where it could do no harm. This tale contains some vital teachings of Taoism. Aiming to harmonise the image of the square of nine chambers with conditions on earth, Yü

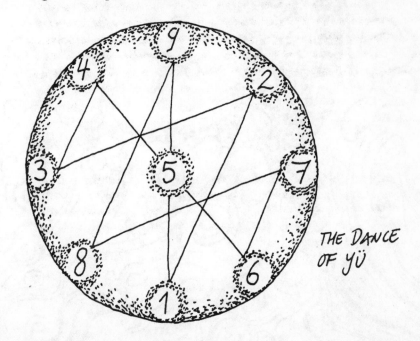

THE DANCE
OF YÜ

the Great divided the land of China into nine districts and established heavenly harmony by giving an enchanted sacrificial cauldron - the sort with three legs that can be used for offerings or as an incense burner - in each part of the land. The nine cauldrons brought peace and fertility to the reborn land.

How the Dance is done

To dance the eight trigrams requires some tricky technical information. As maybe you'll want to do a ritual along these lines one day, I'll give a brief synopsis of the principle of the ceremony and hope that this is not too complicated a task. Plenty of Taoist rites make use of the dance of Yü. First the eight signs are projected on the ground. Look at the illustrations now and you can see that the order of the dance is made up out of the appearance of numbers in a magical square. In the ordinary arrangement, the dance of Yü begins in the north and ends in the south. The dance pattern can be applied to the circle of early and later heaven, that is, the dance steps remain the same but the signs visualized in each direction differ. When you use the circle of early heaven you begin with the receptive and end with the creative, using the circle of later heaven the dance begins with dark water and ends with bright fire. Dancing in the circle of Primal Heaven establishes the heavenly balance of the beginning while a dance in the circle of Later Heaven harmonises the dynamic changes of earth and the order of the seasons.

So far this is a fairly simple matter. Some found it too simple and introduced complications. There are several schools of thunder magic which were developed to counter and combat the malevolent sorceries of the Tao of the left with its violent spirits. In the performance of thunder magic the dance of Yü is a key element. Not the simple version of the dance but a variety that was invented around the fifth century to introduce a bit of exclusive secret knowledge and confusion. In the circle of the eight signs, Ken, the Mountain represents not only a cloud covered peak but also (look at the shape of the sign) the entrance of a cave. In this aspect, the sign receives the title 'The Gate of Life' and becomes a crucial focus of power. In the usual arrangement of the chart of the later heaven, the sign Ken is in the northeast. The thunder magicians, however, decided that the position of the gate is not fixed but changes every few hours. In their system the gate of the otherworld has to be found.

The position of this gate depends on the constellation known as the Great Bear (Ursa major), also called the Big Dipper or the Great Wagon. If you look at it as a wagon, you can see that the shaft points in a certain direction. As the wagon moves around the polar star, the direction of the shaft keeps changing. If the shaft points at the east, for instance, the gate to the otherworld is also in the east. This means that the eastern trigram functions as the gate. This does not refer to the real direction east, but works as follows: imagine a circle around a wagon. Above the wagon is south and below it, north, while east and west are to the sides. As the wagon keeps moving, there is a new gate every couple of hours. It's part of the complications in ritual thunder magic Taoism to calculate the direction of the gate. In practice, the gate shifts from trigram to trigram as the great bear moves around the centre of heaven.

The gate represents the weakest and most dangerous point in the circle, as it seems strong on the outside but is weak further in. You might argue that the sign Kun, the receptive, is a lot weaker than Ken. Though this is true, a Chinese strategist would not dream of attacking at a spot where an attack is expected. Weak as Kun is, it might conceal an ambush. Ken, looking strong but being weak, is a much better choice. At this sign, the otherworld is closest. The dangerous Chia spirits use it to come to earth, so do various disease spirits, and generally, people fear to lose their vital Ch'i energy through this gate. The deceased leave earth through this doorway, but they also use this gate to escape from hell and to ascend to heaven. It is also the point where the thunder magic Taoist begins and ends the dance of Yü, and from which the power of the thunder-breath is summoned. Sealing this dangerous place is among the first priorities of the practising ritualist.

Imagine that you place the square of Yü in the centre of the circle. If you place 1 at the gate-trigram you proceed to dance to 2, then 3 and so on until you arrive at 1 again. Then the gate is shifted round the circle and the dance is repeated. A shift of 30 degrees, and twelve repetitions, seals the twelve directions of space. A shift of 45 degrees and nine repetitions, seals the gates of the eight trigrams. Continue with this until you have performed the dance nine times, and the circle

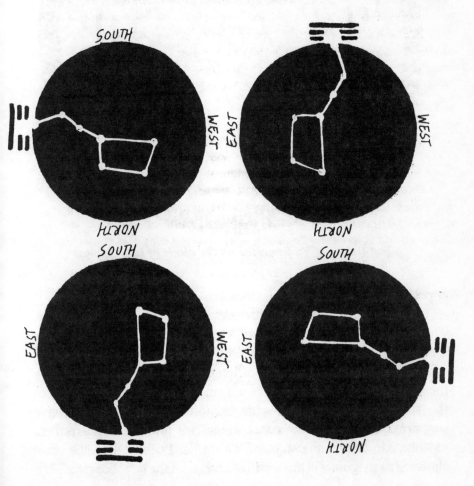

The Dance of Yu projected on the circle of later heaven

is perfectly protected from all sides.

Other versions require that the dance is performed twelve times. This is the case when the dance of Yü is used at the end of a three or five day Chiao ritual. As Michael Saso describes more fully, the chief cantor enters the ritual space bearing the Shu Wen memorial. The memorial is a rescript that grants the prayers of the community, frees the souls from hell and awards immortality to those who have supported the ritual. This dance completes the ritual and restores balance. He dances the steps of Yü on the Lo Shu, i.e. the chart showing the trigrams in the world of change of the later heaven. Then the high priest receives the memorial in the centre of the circle. He summons the power of thunder and dances the Ho T'u, i.e. the eight signs in their early heaven arrangement, the circle of permanence and stability. This dance is repeated twelve times, once for each month. In this rite, he starts at the north, the receptive, earth, and proceeds to wind then to fire and so on. Work it out on the chart and think it through.

Primarily, the dance of Yü functions not only as an exorcism sealing the circle. It also has the effect of bringing the divine influence of heaven to earth, and of balancing and harmonising conditions in the material world. The same effect can be found in the microcosmos, as health and wholeness is restored in the ritualist.

In practical Taoist magic, the eight signs offer access to a wide range of energies and consciousness states. While the gate of life and death is of great importance in establishing the circle, for practical matters other signs may be utilized. In fact each of the eight signs can function as a gate, and each of them is guarded by a jade girl spirit, who '*carries messages and scatters flowers*'. You can find access to the energies of the eight signs by using them as gates.

The wonderful *Pingyaozhuan*, written by Luo Guanzhong and extended by Feng Menglong, gives some examples of the use of these gates. In one episode, a Taoist adept makes rain at an altar standing in the north of the circle, the direction of water. After some spells and secret hand-gestures, he opens a small gourd vessel (this may symbolize opening an alchemical oven or vessel in the body) and, using a fan, allows a black vapour to ascend to the height of the ninth heaven, where it becomes a dark cloud covering the earth. Then he turns to a black paper-dragon, wakes it, and sends it winging to the sky. The dragon opens the cloud and soon lightning flashes and heavy raindrops fall.

The other directions offer different energy vapours, which are often used for meditative alchemy and the transformation of the Taoist. In the east, you can find the green-blue vapour of wood/wind, ruled by the

Green Emperor, our old friend Fu Hsi. To the south is the red energy of fire, guarded by the Red Emperor, Shennong. West is the white energy of metal and precious stones, its ruler is the White Emperor Shao Hao, whose descendants had only a single eye, straight in the middle of the brow. In the north is the energy of water and wintertime. Its colour is black and its guardian is the Black Emperor Chuan Hsü, whose mother was a water goddess. He had three monstrous sons (each of them had three heads) and only one humanoid one, the unlucky Kun who could not stop the flood. In the centre of the circle is the yellow realm of earth, governed by the Yellow Emperor, Huang Ti. The Yellow Emperor is such an important figure in Chinese legend that you would do well to read up on him. He is the inventor of medicine, writing and metalworking, but also a special patron of all shape-changers. It is said that he became the lord of beasts by wearing their skin and fur and dancing their motions. In his army, all officers had animal names. It might be worth contemplating how the ancient emperors fit the cycle of aeons, and the evolution of humanity.

In this system, each direction offers a specific energy which has the form of a vapour. In the rites of inner alchemy, the Taoist calls forth various vapours and inhales them. They are circulated in the body, refined, blended, stored, and released when desired. Another option is to surround oneself with a colourful vapour, to use it in charging a talisman or to fill a ritual space. Vapours are usually exhaled through the nose, the breath should be smooth and inaudible. Some vapours can be gates of dreaming or astral projection. One method to fly to the height of heaven is to travel on a purple vapour, after you have thoroughly saturated yourself with its essence. In this system, the purple, green and amber (peach) haze may function as gateways to the stars. (See appendix two.)

As these rites are complicated, and I am totally ignorant about their fine details, I hope that these few hints will suffice to make you set out to develop your own methods. You would do well to keep in mind that the five Chinese energies (wind/wood, fire, earth, metal/precious stones and water) are not identical with the Greek elements that appear so central to Western magick, or the yogic lore of the Tattvas. When the Greek philosophers invented their elements, they were trying to work out what matter, and therefore the world, is made of. Their elements have substance.

The Chinese energies seem similar, as they make use of similar symbols, but refer to activity and change. This may be a bit difficult to comprehend. Each of the five Chinese energies is a force that influences and transforms matter, it is not a thing as such and does not belong to the realm of phenomena. Water, for example, refers to some (but not all) aspects of watery behaviour and not necessarily to the substance you encounter in rivers, oceans and bathtubs. Sadly, some early translators have inflicted the name 'elements' on the five energies of the Chinese, giving the mistaken impression that the Greek model is related or at least similar. Lots of people seem to think it is, they are happy to discover something that seems vaguely familiar and instantly stop thinking. If you explain the unknown by means of the known you are not learning anything new.

You can only understand the subtle interaction of the five Chinese energies when you forget the Western interpretation for a while. Even the term 'energies' may mislead. Try to think of them as 'changers' or transformers if you prefer a more dynamic, and less object-bound interpretation. Another good term is 'the five movers', as they induce motion and change. The same sort of mind-frame may well be useful when considering the eight signs. The symbols are just a means of representing energies that are too subtle to be comprehended otherwise.

Exercise Five: Union with the eight signs

How can you use the circles of the eight signs for your magick? One useful approach is to find out which energy you could use at the time being. Maybe you would like to rest patiently like a mountain, or celebrate in the sign of the joyous, or become light and inspired in the sign of wood and wind. Maybe you could do with a boost of creative energy, or maybe you would like to relax in the sign of the receptive. Perhaps you already know what energy would do you good, but if you don't you can easily find out by consulting the oracle. Imagine that you want to become calm and still. This sort of experience can be found in the sign Ken, Keeping Still, mountain. Imagine the circle of later heaven on the ground. Step into the middle and turn so that you face the northeast. First you can contact the mountain by visualizing its sign. Make it an impressive vision - by now you should know how an image can be represented in order to make it vivid and impressive to you. If you don't, dare to experiment. Bring the vision close to you. How close does it have to be to produce a strong effect? Make it large, if you like, add strong colours and clear contrasts and so on.

Add sound and feeling, smell and taste, and make this vision a full experience for all senses. Allow your mind to show you all sorts of great mountain ranges and whatever else you associate with the sign. When the representation is fully developed and arouses a distinct sensation of presence you are ready to unite with it. For a start you could visualize the essence of the sign in the form of a colourful vapour. Standing before the sign you can draw the vapour into your lungs and radiate it through your body. You can literally soak in this energy and feel it saturate every cell of your being.

When you experience yourself in harmony with the essence of the mountain, spin around and step forward into the sign. As you turn to face the centre of the circle you have assumed the place and function of the mountain. The important element is that you identify with the energy and sentience of your sign. The closer you identify, the closer you associate with the vision, the more real will your experience be and the more fully will it transform and refine you. Sometimes this can mean lucid visions. Sometimes it can involve strong feelings, or new ideas. Don't expect anything specific. For one thing, this sort of shape-shifting requires a bit of practice to function with ease, and for another, a useful transformation is not always a dramatic one.

Plenty of beginners in magick think that the great and passionate events are the ones that produce the greatest changes. If you subscribe to this view you'll depend on dramatic measures to get things done. Now drama can be nice, especially to convince beginners that something strong is happening. The dramatic approach, however, is just one way among many. It is by no means stronger than other forms of magick, but then you may need a bit of refinement to realize the value of subtle techniques. Some of the most important changes can be induced without any drama. They may be so subtle that the conscious mind does not even notice that anything is happening, and this is an excellent state, as an ignorant conscious mind won't feel tempted to meddle and interfere.

Returning to our rite, you are on your own now. You can enjoy the energy of each sign for as long as you like. You can store it in your body. You can take it along as you go for a walk or close your eyes and make it the gate of dreams. You can become the energy and use it to charge ritual objects, talismans and fetishes. Whatever you do, at some time you'll wish to end the ritual. This is the occasion to release the accumulated energy. First of all, give your thanks to the gods, spirits and sentiences involved in the rite. They are you and you are them and you have all done a lot for yourself. Spin around and leap into the centre of the circle. Turn around and face the sign of Mountain, Standing Still, where you have been a moment before. Hold out your hands to the sign and release the energy excess into its source. As you exhale you can visualize the mountain power returning to its origin. Then bend over until your hands touch the ground. Exhaling, allow the last remnants of excessive mountain power to rush out of your flesh through arms and legs and into the waiting depths below. Do this until you are in balance with yourself. By the way, standing on one leg is a good way of testing if one has earthed the energy properly. Rub your belly for a while, bring the rite to an end and depart. If you want more details on the art of earthing energy, you can find them in *Helrunar* and *Seidways*.

Aggressive magick

There is also an aggressive mode of using the system of the eight signs, which became popular among the military sorcerers of left hand Tao. In ancient China, martial arts and Taoist sorcereries were often combined, and generals were expected to be masters of military strategy as well as fighting magic. In this school, there are a number of secret titles for the eight signs, you read them earlier. There is also a set of attributions to military activity (see Saso 1978).

Chien is 'experienced battle-trained soldiers. Attack!'
Kan is 'hidden soldiers. Ambush.'
Chen is 'reserve army',
Sun is 'reinforcements',
Li is 'thunder-brigade, penetrate deeply',
Kun is 'defensive army, protect and defend' and
Tui is 'an army of heroes, protect and defend'.

Ken, the gate, is missing in M. Saso′s study.

When the circle is perfectly established, it can be opened and transformed into a serpent. The head of the snake is the sign of the creative, Chien. The priest invokes a Chia spirit - a not totally harmless task as the Chia spirits have an enormous amount of chaotic and often destructive energy at their disposal - and becomes obsessed. In this state, the priest transforms into the head of the serpent and sets out to work evil. Luckily, most Taoists refrain from such exercises of their power. Mastering the Chia spirits implies that one masters the unstable forces which they represent, and in doing so, the desire to work destructive sorceries tends to evaporate. Though I haven't found any references to other uses of this serpent conjuration in literature, I would like to ask the readers to think about this matter. Surely there must be other rites that can be worked in serpent shape? How about using it to banish, or to consecrate a ritual space? Or assuming the form while going for a nice long walk? Can the mood of the serpent be changed when one opens the circle at another point so that a different trigram forms the head? Ask your spirits and find out.

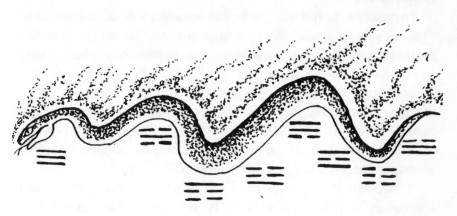

Stellar lore

Of course there are many other equally interesting lists of attributions to the eight signs. It might be worth considering that there is plenty of evidence supporting the theory that originally, Taoism was a stellar cult. One variety of it, popular to this day in several Asian countries, is the cult of the nine imperial gods. These nine deities are the sons of the goddess of the polar star, Tou Mu (Doumu). No doubt the number nine reminds you of the nine cells in the magical square of Yü the Great. It also corresponds to the seven stars of the constellation Ursa Major, the Great Bear, or the Big Dipper, which you have already encountered as the stellar sign showing the direction of the Gate of Life and Death. This sign is one of the easiest to find in the nightsky. It is visible all the year round (for inhabitants of the northern hemisphere) and it looks just like Lao Tsu's eyebrows. The ancient Chinese astronomers were well aware that Ursa Major consists of more than seven stars, but they decided to attribute only seven of them, the most easily visible ones, to the imperial gods. Well, with seven stars you can hardly house nine stellar gods.

To make up the full nine, two other stars had to be added to the list. Their exact nature is not that easy to determine. One myth claims that the two missing stars are actually invisible to human eyes but are easy to see with the eyes of an immortal. Probably some wandering immortal told this likely story to the founders of the cult, and proposed that the two invisible stars are stars that signify change and transformation. A text of the Sung dynasty offers another explanation and informs us that the two stars are not invisible but happen to be The Sustainer (Alcor) and Far Flight (Bootes).

A medieval treatise replaces Far Flight with Straightener, a star supposedly attached to Phecta. It is an invisible star and it's also known as Void. Yet another mythical theory balances the nine stars of the imperial gods with a series of nine stars that radiate a light that does not shine. These are also invisible to mortal eyes and house nine goddesses who are the consorts of the imperial gods. The concept of invisible stars comes remarkably close to the modern idea of Black Holes and similar phenomena.

While these theories sound like a lot of useless speculation, there were actually Taoists who made use of their practical implications. The goddesses of the nine dark stars, for instance, could be invoked in order to turn the ritualist invisible. The sign of Ursa Major had further uses. If you imagine it as a spoon or ladle you have four stars forming a bowl and three stars that form the handle. The bowl can be ritually placed over the head in order to protect a person, and a visualization exercise attributed to the adepts of Mao Shan elaborates on this idea. The adept goes to sleep under the bowl of the Dipper, that is, the bowl covers the head and torso while the handle protects and covers the legs. When this visualization is firmly established, the nine imperial gods are invoked by name and secret title. Then the radiant essence of the stars comes out of the vision and drenches the sleeper with its subtle energy. This practice is supposed to refine and transform its adepts who may eventually become immortal.

Of course each of the nine stars has its attributions. Eight of them have a trigram to represent their influence, and all of them are assigned to the system of the five movers. For more details on this complicated cosmology, see the works of Michael Saso and Ruth-Inge Heinze. There is a great deal of highly elaborate stellar lore in the sorceries of the darksome Tao of the Left, but it would go far beyond the purpose of this essay to comment on it. Suffice it to say that there are 28 constellations invoked in its rituals, each of them symbolized by a beast spirit.

Eight signs and the body

Another system of attributions relates the eight signs to the organs of the body, while yet another system of meditation proposes that the signs refer to energy centres of the subtle body. These are similar to the well known *chakras* of the Indian Yoga traditions, but differ widely where it comes to locating them. The more important Hindu chakras follow the human spine. So do some of the Chinese, but unlike the Indian gnosis, the Taoist centres are arranged in a circle. The Ch'i current flows up from the perineum along the spine, up and around the head and down along the front of the body and back to the perineum continuously. The Indian notion that energy/sentience could permanently ascend to the 'higher centres' is impossible in the Taoist model, where energies go round and round in eternal transformation. More data on this system of visualization can be found in the next chapter. The eight trigrams, once associated with various power zones, become a useful vocabulary for the practice of these meditations.

Exercise Six: Magick of guesture

The nine chambers of the dance of Yü can also be projected on the digits of the left hand. Perhaps I should clarify this method a bit. A lot of Taoist sorceries make use of obscure mudras, many of them so secret that the hand that forms them is hidden in the sleeve of the ritual robe. One of the mudra-systems is based on the 'magical square' invented by Yü. You simply imagine the numbers on the digits of index, middle and ring-finger of the left hand until the associations are quite clear in your memory.

Next, go fully into the consciousness of one of the eight signs. Press the proper digit with your thumb while you imagine the sign, its energy and meaning, and increase pressure as you go more fully into the experience. This meditation 'anchors' the feeling of pressure on a specific location to the desired consciousness. Proceed with this until all nine chambers are distinctly associated with the eight signs and the middle. This may take a couple of days if done thoroughly. The use of this meditation is to produce a series of points-of-access. You can dance the whole series of trigrams with this method, simply moving your thumb from finger to finger. Also, you may use this mudra-map to invoke all sorts of consciousness-states.

There are, by the way, several such maps being used in ritual Taoism. Another one projects the twelve signs of the Chinese zodiac on the twelve digits of four fingers, which goes to show that systems of cosmology are there to be used practically.

The oracle script of the Shang dynasty inscribed on tortoise shells and animal bones.

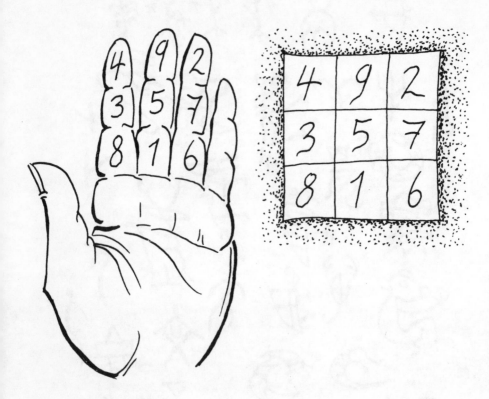

The eight signs and the martial arts

The eight signs were influential on many aspects of Chinese culture. There is a martial arts system, Pa Kua Chuan (Eight Signs Boxing) that has the practitioner walk around an imaginary circle of trigrams while performing all sorts of hand and feet techniques. This is not far from the use of martial arts in public Taoist ritual. Certain ceremonies, such as blessing the neighbourhood, driving evil disease spirits away or the Chiao rituals of renewal and union involve public activity. This may include drawing sigils into the air with a sword, scaring demons with trumpets or the exorcistic use of a snake form (a rather esoteric but also extremely violent martial arts style) to clear up the ritual space.

The eight signs and the ritual calendar

Leaving the magical and turning to the religious, we can find the influence of the seasons (as in the chart of later heaven) exert itself on the rituals practised by the emperor and his court. According to Lü Bu We's invaluable ritual calendar, the Son of Heaven had a specific dwelling place during each of the twelve months.

The four sides of the 'Hall of Light' were named after the four seasons, that is:

east	=	the green force of yang,
south	=	the bright hall,
west	=	general beauty and
north	=	the dark hall.

The hall itself was divided into nine chambers, and the emperor moved around from month to month to stay in harmony with the cycle of the year.

Likewise, the colours of the directions influenced the choice of clothing. During the three months of spring, members of the court were required to dress in green and to wear green jewellery. In summer, it was red, in autumn white and in winter black. More so, each season had its specific dishes, sacrifices, horses, flags etc., and required certain forms of behaviour. All of these were essential to keep the emperor, as the representative of heaven, in harmony with the changeful conditions here on earth and vice versa. The way of heaven is round, consequently, the way of the emperor is also round, or as Huang Ti (quoted by Lü Bu We) said: *'The ruler may not have a specific place. If he has a place, he has no place'*.

Numbers in divination

So far, so good. Maybe these lines will suffice to inspire you to develop some interesting new magical methods, or to examine your own system in the light of another one. Magick is, after all, more than the art of curing pimples and banishing evil influences. If you approach magick as a user, a couple of simple spells and remedies in whatever system will be enough to keep you happy. If you really want to make an art and science out of it, studies in other systems of magick are essential. It is only when you feel at home in several magical systems that you'll begin to understand just what is local tradition and what constitutes the essential structure of belief and consciousness.

Those of you who like to practise *I Ching* divination using the concept of the 'changing lines' may perhaps enjoy to combine it with the visionary method you developed earlier. This is a complicated matter that suits some people perfectly while being useless for others.

For a start, we could examine how it works. A hexagram consists of six lines which are arranged on top of each other. Two symbols, i.e. the open yin (- -) and the closed yang line (—), are sufficient to produce a total of 64 hexagrams, and this is an extensive vocabulary to express a suitable answer. Some diviners evidently did not think so.

Let's look at history. The first sinologists trying to figure out the evolution of the *I Ching* assumed that complicated things develop out of simple ones. They fancied that sometime in Neolithic China, some enterprising soul invented divination using the primal symbols of yin and yang, which were interpreted as, say, yes and no, or maybe auspicious and unlucky. If this hypothesis is true, the two lines of yin and yang are the oldest elements of the *I Ching* and the foundation of all future development and complexity. We find a certain support for this assumption in the legend of Fu Hsi. The Green Emperor, as myth has it, did not only invent the eight trigrams but also a system of writing making use of knotted strings. Though little is known about its use, it might be worth considering if the yin and yang lines were the graphical expression of a string with and without a knot. Not bad for a simple theory, and a bit more refined than the school of thought claiming the yin and yang lines are abstract forms of the human genitalia.

The theory, so far, seemed eminently satisfactory, until archaeological finds turned it upside down. As it turned out, some of the tortoise-shell lots and bones used for oracular purposes starting with the Shang and Chou period showed graphical designs. These were not words but symbols signifying numbers. These numbers were written on top of each other, and produced tri- or hexagrams. Mind you, these tri- and hexagrams did not make use of the yin and yang lines in use today. In fact, it took the archaeologists years of research before they recognised them as tri- and hexagrams at all! In keeping with what is known of early Chinese numerology, the even numbers signified the yin lines while the odd numbers signified yang.

In the earliest period we know of, the numbers 1, 5, 6, 7 and 8 were used to describe a hexagram, the number 6 appearing with unusual frequency. In the next phase, from the eighth to fifth century BCE, the oracular bones favoured the numbers 1, 5, 6, 8, 9. A later form of divination, making use of bamboo lots, used the numbers 1, 6, 8, and 9, while hexagrams on a clay vessel of the Chou period were written using the numbers 1, 5, 6, and 8. While it is not certain that these ancient oracles had exactly the same meaning as the *I Ching*, they do point at a wide range of alternative systems.

The form of the *I Ching* you are acquainted with makes use of the numbers 6, 7, 8 and 9. This works as follows. Lets look at the classical use of the three coin oracle.

Each coin has a yin and a yang side. The yin side counts 2 (an even number) and the yang side 3. When you toss three coins at once, the sum will be among the numbers 6, 7, 8 and 9. Yin, yin and yin (2+2+2) equals 6. Yang, yang and yang (3+3+3) equals 9.

6 is an even number, thus, a yin line is drawn.

9 is an odd number, and yields a yang line.

Yin, yin and yang (2+2+3) equals 7, an odd number, so the line you draw is yang.

Yang, yang and yin (3+3+2) equals 8; as an even number, 8 produces a yin line.

As you can see, there are two ways of having a yin, and two ways of having a yang line.

In fact, there are two sorts of them. A yin line that consists entirely of yin (as in 6) is so extreme that it becomes unstable. A yang line consisting entirely of yang (9) is just as extreme, and likely to change.

This is one of the key-concepts of Taoism.

Phenomena which become one-sided and extreme tend to turn into their opposites. Thus, the 6 and the 9 refer to 'moving lines' in the hexagram, lines which will soon transform. A moving yin line becomes a normal yang line, a moving yang line becomes a normal yin line in due course. The numbers 7 (yang) and 8 (yin) are stable, that is, you draw them and they remain as they are. If you use the method of the three coins, or the yarrow stalks, your answer is a hexagram which will in all likeliness contains some moving lines. First you should study the hexagram. Then draw a second one by changing the moving lines into their opposites. This second hexagram reveals how the situation is likely to develop. As each hexagram may at least theoretically turn into every other hexagram, this equips your deep mind with a total of 64 x 63 answers.

The moving lines

In the classical *I Ching* text, a considerable amount of space is dedicated to a detailed commentary on the moving lines. This commentary is traditionally ascribed to the Duke of Chou, though linguistic analysis shows that most of it comes from the eighth century BCE and later periods. Each of the six levels of a hexagram can house a moving line. Perhaps you would like to include these details in your divination. You could use the easy way, and look up the meaning of each moving line in the good book. If you have come this far, however, you might as well do some thinking on your own.

There is a hidden structure to the lines. Each hexagram consists of six levels. Like the trigrams, these six levels can be identified with the three realms of heaven, humanity and earth. In this case, the two bottom lines correspond to earth and the underworlds, the two middle lines to the middle world of humans and living beings, and the two top lines to the height of heaven. This structure may give you some insights.

As you may remember, the basic system of Chinese numerology claims that the yin numbers are even and the yang numbers odd. Take a look at a hexagram now. The first line drawn is always the bottom line, so that the hexagram grows from bottom to the top. As the bottom level is the first, it corresponds with the number 1 and the quality of yang. The second level, being of an even number, corresponds with yin, the third with yang, the fourth with yin, the fifth with yang and the sixth with yin. If you have a yin line in the first place, i.e. in a level

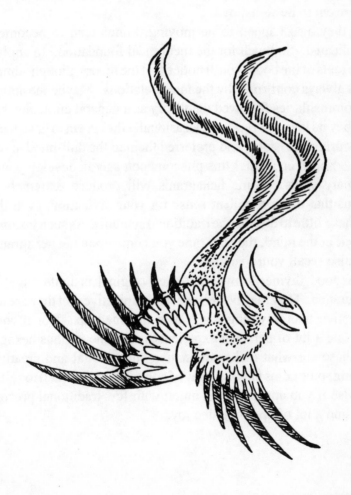

associated with yang energy, this yin line is neither strong nor influential. If it is a moving yin line, its influence is considerably strengthened, which may or may not be a good thing. If you have a yang line in the first place, this yang is powerful, as it is yang strengthened by a yang position. A moving yang line in the first place is stronger still, and may influence the meaning of the whole divination. Is this clear? Basically, the idea is that yin lines in yin positions, and yang lines in yang positions have a strong and beneficial influence, while yang lines in yin positions and yin lines in yang positions don't seem to be so happy.

If they also happen to be moving, things tend to become a bit complicated. So much for the theoretical foundation. In applying it to the texts of the book, you'll notice that the theory, though admirable, is not always confirmed by the interpretations. Maybe the authors of the commentaries followed the theory as a general guideline, but did not obey its laws too rigidly. Occasionally they seem to have had their really original visions, and preferred them to the dull-minded regulations. You'll encounter this phenomenon as you develop your own visionary skills. Some hexagrams will produce extremely vivid visions that make excellent sense for your divination, even though they have little to do with the traditional symbols. As such visions tend to stick in the mind, the next time you come upon the hexagram, you may also recall your vision.

A good diviner knows that such original insights ought to be encouraged. They may be personal and subjective, but they are no less subjective than anything King Wen dreamed up. You'll come to associate a lot of personal experiences with the various hexagrams, and these are what makes divination such a vital and creative art. Tossing some coins may be a way of communing from self to self. You are wise if you approach this union with few traditional preconceptions and a lot of open-minded joy.

Appendix One: I Ching - recent discoveries

This brings us to the final section. So far, I hope that you have found everything more or less comprehensible, and have enjoyed working your divination. In order to keep things from becoming too easy I would like to introduce you to some recent developments in the study of the *I Ching*.

I Ching prehistory

The admirable translations of Legge and Wilhelm have done much to make the *Book of Changes* available to Western audiences. In the past decades, the good book has almost attained the status of a cult, and has become an integral part of the hippie and new-age movements. Some over-enthusiastic authors have called it 'the oldest book of humanity', and have happily exaggerated its age by thousands of years. This seems a fairly typical reaction. Whenever something mysterious and Asian is to be sold to the Western world, you can be certain that thousands of years of age are attributed to it. In fact, one might get the impression that none of the Asian cultures has developed anything new over the last centuries, nor that anything has been improved over the millennia.

Silly as it may seem, people love things of great age, provided they come from far-off exotic places. With the *I Ching*, the same has happened. Once people read that the oldest commentaries were written by King Wen around 1150BCE, they take up this bit of traditional lore and see it as proof that the entire text is of a similar age. Quite a few early translators contributed to this myth and treated the text as if it were the work of two or three authors. Worse yet, the countless readers who tossed a few coins and looked up the answer (usually without bothering to read all the difficult bits) soon found that the oracle works, and venerated the text as holy writ. Luckily, during the last decades there has been a lot of new research. New insights have come up, new questions have been asked and some aged fables have been demolished. All of this took place outside of the popular attention. As I believe that any good magical or divinatory system can profit from new insights and interpretations, I shall now proceed to annoy you with some unusual ideas.

Let us look at the text as we know it. Some of it is attributed to King Wen and his son the Duke of Chou. This does not mean that the *I Ching* you see in the bookshop today is actually their original work. Linguistic analysis shows clearly that most of the passages were not composed around 1150BCE but much later. The text may have seen the influence of dozens of authors, it even includes quotations from other works, lines from poetry and folk songs and a number of proverbial sayings. And far from coming from bronze-age China, the version of the *I Ching* you are familiar with comes from the Tang period and goes back to a compilation by Lu Deming (550-630 CE). Up to quite recently, this version was the oldest complete copy of the *I Ching*.

How is it that this work has gained such a reputation for venerable old age? A book written around 600 CE is not quite as old as some would have it. There is, luckily, some evidence for the *I Ching* from earlier periods.

In 1922 the 'stone classics' were discovered. These were a collection of books which had been copied on 64 huge stone slabs around the year 175 CE. The emperor Lingdi had ordered these inscriptions, possibly in order to produce a standard text version of the Confucian classics, which could be copied by scholars. Sadly, most of the stone-books were soon destroyed in a war, so that the excavators only found some fragments of this older version of the *I Ching*. These fragments showed some divergence from the standard text, but most of them could be explained as spelling errors and the like. Other emperors took up the same idea and had the *I Ching* engraved on stone, so that the archaeologists managed to compile about 10% of the full text from independent sources. Most of the material seemed to support the authenticity of the full text.

In 1977, several hundred inscriptions on bamboo and wood were discovered in Anhui. These included the text of forty hexagrams and are dated around 165 BCE. Tough luck that a lot of these texts showed marked differences to the *I Ching* that we know it. So far, these texts remain unpublished.

Things got more interesting when a mound was opened in Mawangdui, near Changsha, in the province of Hunan. The mound contained the graves of a noble named Li Cang and his wife, Lady Dai. It also contained a grave of a mysterious person who had been buried without a name plate in the year 165 BCE. This anonymous corpse was clearly a person of some importance. His equipment for the otherworld included various weapons and military equipment as well as some excellent maps. Better still, there was a large chest in the tomb which contained more than fifty books. These had been carefully written on silk. Among the books was an excellent collection of historical and political treatises, works on medicine, astronomical tables, a work on horses, the oldest known texts on pulse-diagnosis and Ch'i kung exercises, studies on astrology and divination as well as a selection of Taoist classics. These included instructions on life-extension (not that useful, considering that the deceased had died at the age of thirty), works attributed to the Yellow Emperor and two different versions of the *Tao Te Ching*. Another text, entitled *Punishment and Virtue* exists in three versions. Obviously, the owner of this library appreciated having important literature in several versions.

Most important for our topic, the tomb included, what is, so far, the oldest complete version of the *I Ching*. This should have caused a sensation, if the work had been easier to digest. As it was, the Mawangdui *I Ching* contained such a lot of independence from the standard text that most scholars were not happy with it at all.

For a start, the order of the hexagrams differs. Where the standard version shows the hexagrams in pairs, but has no meta-structure to organize the pairs, the Mawangdui version has a neat and precise organization. The hexagrams appear in groups of eight. In the first group, all eight signs have Chien as the top trigram, the second Ken, then Kan, Chen, Kun, Tui, Li and Sun. In each group, the bottom trigrams follow the order Chien, Kun, Ken, Tui, Kan, Li, Chen and

Sun. As Dominique Hertzer has demonstrated in her study, this pattern follows an arrangement of the earlier heaven which agrees with certain Mawangdui commentaries, but differs from the standard text. If you like, you could draw two circles based on these arrangements and study them, preferably in a gentle trance state.

The structure of the Mawangdui version is closely related to the trigrams themselves. Unlike the classical version, the Mawangdui text shows each hexagram as a combination of two trigrams (there is a gap between lines three and four). The yang lines look as expected, but the yin lines are drawn in a form similar to the Chinese number eight. Examination of the text reveals that about a quarter of the characters differ from the standard version. This was certainly bad news for the traditionalists.

Before we can examine some of these differences with regard to the trigrams, it might be useful to consider the problems inherent in ancient Chinese literature. As you probably know, Chinese writing takes the forms of pictograms while the spoken language has to make do with a rather limited number of syllables. To make the most of these syllables, there are several ways of pronouncing each of them. You can say a syllable in Mandarin with a rising or falling accent, or with an accent that rises and falls, or falls and rises again. Each of these versions has an entirely different meaning, and each of them is written with a different character. In daily life, this means that a speaker has to take great care to pronounce properly, and that the hearer is obliged to make sense out of a word by considering the context.

A similar sound can mean a lot of different things. In Chinese thought and custom, the similarities are often meaningful. The word for 'bat' (Fu) sounds much like the word for 'luck' (Fu), and so you can find little abstract bats on Chinese dishes and teacups, which are certain to bring good luck. Likewise, the number four (Szu) sounds similar to the word for death, which can make it an unlucky omen to seat four people at a table.

Chinese is full of these obscure associations, and the literati of the past made full use of them to add several layers of meaning to their works. Sadly, such double, triple and quadruple meanings cannot be translated into most languages. As a result, all of Chinese literature, as soon as it is translated, becomes a simplified version that lacks a lot of the original ambiguity. This applies to modern texts but even more so to works of antiquity. Two-thousand years ago, the Chinese language had not yet settled down into a standard system of writing, and similar sounding syllables were occasionally written with different characters.

More complicated yet, there were a number of taboo-words which were avoided during certain periods, and replaced with words that sounded differently, but had a similar meaning. This makes each attempt to read or translate an old text something of a hopeful reconstruction.

In the Mawangdui *I Ching*, as mentioned before, about a quarter of the characters differ from the standard version. Most of them are pronounced much like the words in the standard version, and so it was an easy matter to explain them as misspellings, which would be quite logical if the text was written according to the spoken words. Most scholars seem to have stopped there. The differences were explained away and their altered meaning was generally ignored. This may give you some estimation of the respect that the standard version of the *I Ching* enjoys among Chinese and Western scholars. Though the Mawangdui *I Ching* is almost a thousand years older than the standard version, it was still believed to be in error.

The 'elder' *I Ching*

It is one of the great virtues of Dominique Hertzer's work (perhaps the only reliable translation of the Mawangdui *I Ching* in a Western language) that she examined the text with an open mind and published it side by side with the well-known Richard Wilhelm translation.

The result is a 'new' *I Ching* full of hitherto unexpected meanings. In regard to the trigrams, the Mawangdui version does not offer such neat commentaries as the *Great Treatise* of the standard version. Or maybe it does, but we'll have to wait for them, as a large amount of the Mawangdui books have not , so far, been published. Be that as it may, we can deduce a lot about the nature of the trigrams when we study the hexagrams which consist of double trigrams. In the following section, some of the names employed are in the pinyin transcription, which differs from the accustomed transcription somewhat. I shall first give the text according to the well known Wilhelm/Baynes version and then add an English version of Dominique Hertzer's translation into German. Those readers who can read German are well advised to read her work in the original.

The first double trigram we encounter in the Mawangdui version is the sign Jian, also known as Chien. Both the standard text and the Mawangdui version give it as the first hexagram. It consists of two Chien trigrams on top of each other. While the Wilhelm version only offers '*The creative works sublime success, furthering through perseverance*' the Mawangdui version according to Hertzer yields:

> '*The lock, the beginning, the growth, the ripeness and the enduring. The star Jian (shines), if one prepares a great cooked meal for an offering this is of auspicious designation.*'

The sign Jian, starting the Mawangdui text, sounds like the word Chien of the standard version but is written differently. This could be a spelling mistake, but how likely is it that a sacred text begins with a mistake in the very first word? It means the bolt that closes and opens a gate, or the handle of a sacrificial vessel, and can generally be used as a word for a lock or a key. Note that the terms beginning, growth, ripeness and endurance may reflect a cycle, such as the four seasons.

Most of the moving lines refer to the motion of a dragon, or the constellation of the dragon, as it moves from the deep to the height.

Hexagram 9 of the Mawangdui version is called Gen and shows two Ken trigrams. In the standard version, this is hexagram 52 called Ken, keeping still, mountain. Wilhelm says:

> *'Keeping still. Keeping his back still so that he no longer feels his body. He goes into his courtyard and does not see his people. No blame.'*

These lines could be a reference to meditative practices. In the Mawangdui version:

> *'The star root (of heaven), it (. . .) rainwater does not run down the body, one goes walking in one's courtyard and (. . .) this/ these human/s not, there is no loss.'*

Here the text was not entirely intact. However, you can see that it refers to the star 'root of heaven' (Gen). The form of the trigram may remind you of a root (firm above the surface, flexible in the deep), but it could also signify the strong influence of a star (top level yang) shedding its subtle influences. Or maybe you would prefer the picture of an umbrella or a waterproof cloak, both of which work wonders when it comes to keeping rainwater from your back. Dominique Hertzer suggests that the star Gen is another term for the second lunar house, called Di, or root. When its stars are visible, a period of drought is said to ensue.

A doubling of the sign Kan, the abysmal, is seen in hexagram 17 of the Mawangdui text, called Xigan. In the standard version, this is hexagram 29, called K'an. Wilhelm's translation reads:

> *'The abysmal repeated. If you are sincere, you have success in your heart, and whatever you do succeeds.'*

While this may be nice to hear, it does not really tell us anything new. By the way, in the (German) translation, the text reads *'If you are truthful. . .'* In dealing with abysses and the like, this makes a lot of difference, as any practising magician could tell you.

The Mawangdui text uses the character Gan which reads *'a gift, an offering, a tribute'*. The text, according to Hertzer, says:

> *'One is to offer a tribute, it gives an answer, "offering the heart of a swallow makes the action successful."'*

Generally, the swallow was a sign of good luck, joy, harmony and success in ancient China. All six moving lines refer to the dangers inherent in offering tribute. How dangerous this may be can be understood if you consider that the state of Changsha, though being officially part of the Han empire, barely managed to retain its independence and its own king in the days when the tomb library was written. The *I Ching* was not just a book for personal fortune telling but was frequently consulted in political matters.

Our next hexagram, consisting of the double Chen, the

arousing, thunder, is number 25 of the Mawangdui version and 51 of the standard text. Wilhelm translated the text as:

> *'Shock brings success. Shock comes - oh, oh! Laughing words -*
> *ha, ha! The shock terrifies for a hundred miles, and he does not*
> *let fall the sacrificial spoon and chalice.'*

The Mawangdui text, translated by Hertzer reads:

> *'At the waking of spring one makes an offering. Spring begins*
> *at new moon (. . .) one says "ya- ya", the beginning of spring*
> *is worshipped everywhere, one does not forget the golden*
> *sacrificial spoon and the sacrificial meat.'*

These two texts have much in common. Traditionally, the season of spring is associated with thunderstorms, and during the first thunderstorm of the year the Taoist goes out to breathe the power of thunder and stores it, for use when required, in the living chalice of the body.

If we double the trigram Kun, the receptive, the result is Hexagram 33 (Mawangdui) and Hexagram 2 (standard version). Wilhelm translates the text:

> *'The receptive brings about sublime success, furthering through*
> *the perseverance of a mare. If the superior man undertakes*
> *something and tries to lead, he goes astray; but if he follows he*
> *finds guidance. It is favourable to find friends in the west and*
> *south, to forego friends in the east and north. Quiet persever-*
> *ance brings good fortune.'*

Hertzer's translation of the Mawangdui text:

> *'At the source of a river (or: at the stream) one offers a great*

sacrifice, this is auspicious for the choice of a mare. The noble has something, wherever he goes, first he strays from the way, (but) then he has found (it). For the ruler it is of advantage to find friends in the southwest and to lose friends in the northeast, verify if it is auspicious (for) times of rest.'

As mares, and horses in general were an extremely popular symbol in ancient China, and lots of meanings were attributed to them, I shall merely remark that a mare can be a metaphor for a wife or concubine, but that your guess is as good as mine. In some periods, horses were yin, in others yang, and when you really think about it, horses are horses.

Our next double trigram is the hexagram 41 (Mawangdui) called Duo, it corresponds with hexagram 58, Tui, the joyous, of the standard version. The Wilhelm translation states:

'The joyous. Success. Perseverance is favourable.'

In the Mawangdui text the judgement is a bit more elaborate. Hertzer's translation tells us:

'Something is lost, making an offering in the small is of auspicious determination.'

The sign Duo has an entirely different meaning as the joyous sign Tui/Dui. It can mean loss and refer to something that is mislaid, lost or taken by force. Literally, the Chinese character symbolizes *'holding a bird'*. This can also be seen in the trigram. The two yang lines at the bottom are a pair of hands while the yin line on top represents the bird. While it may seem hard to reconcile the joyous lake with the image of losing a bird, there are some subtle connections. Duo/Tui is the sign associated with the season of autumn and the energy of metal. While there is great joy in the splendour of autumn, there is also a profound melancholy as the warm season is 'lost' and winter approaches. In autumn, trees lose their last fruits and berries, and in ancient China people tended to lose their heads as well. After the end of harvest came the time for warfare. Also, in this season, criminals were executed. Both ideas are closely aligned with the force of cold metal. The Mawangdui text reminds me of a martial arts saying: 'A weapon is like a bird. Hold it too tight and you suffocate it, hold it too loosely and it flies away'. The same goes for musical instruments, brushes and pens, tools of all sorts etc., but I'm sure you can think of many other applications such as in human interactions or meditation.

Hexagram 49 of the Mawangdui text is the double sign Luo, corresponding with hexagram 30, Li, the clinging, fire of the standard text. First the Wilhelm translation:

> *'The clinging. Perseverance furthers. It brings success. Care of the cow brings good fortune.'*

The Mawangdui text, as translated by Hertzer, offers the following:

> *'The net (or the state Luo) is of auspicious destiny; for the offering of a sacrifice it is auspicious to breed cows.'*

If you look at the trigram, you can see that the top and bottom lines are strong, but that the middle is soft and yielding, or even has a hole in it. Such an image can be taken to represent a net. The net, though not especially fiery, is like fire in that it holds and clings. The character Luo can also refer to a rope that connects the axle to the cart, or have the meaning of catching, holding and binding. As Dominique Hertzer points out, the sign may also have had a political meaning. The character Luo can represent the state Luo, which was destroyed by the state Chu. Many of the refugees from Luo came to settle in Changsha.

Finally we come to Mawangdui hexagram 57, Suan, which corresponds with hexagram 57 of the standard text, Sun, the gentle, penetrating, wind. In the Wilhelm translation of the standard text we learn:

> *'The gentle. Success through what is small. It furthers one to have somewhere to go. It furthers one to see the great man.'*

Hertzer's translation of the Mawangdui text offers:

> *'(The counting of the) oracular stalks, (. . .) a sacrifice is offered, it is beneficial when there is something that can be done, it is beneficial to see a great human.'*

The character Suan refers to the counting of the yarrow stalks for oracular purposes. There seem to have been several systems of doing so. In the comments to three moving lines the Mawangdui text refers to the act of counting the stalks *'under the bed'* which could be a metaphor for working the divination with great secrecy. Originally, the character Suan used to mean rods that were used to calculate years. From this meaning, it came to be used for any sort of calculation, including the counting of the yarrow stalks. Chinese literature occasionally mentions *'the numbers of heaven'*. These predestine fate, length of life, encounters with important people and coincidental events. Far from being fixed, such 'fatal' numbers can be recalculated when the Jade Emperor or some other heavenly worthy decides to influence things a bit. The general mood of the hexagram is that of mobility, and this is not far from the motion of the wind through the forest.

How do you like these new insights? A considerable number of scholars and historians, especially those who feel ethically committed to the standard version of the *I Ching*, are not too happy about the existence of the Mawangdui versions. Some seriously ponder if the standard text is invalidated by the existence of the alternative version, and solve the problem by blaming the Mawangdui version for being full of spelling errors. The fact remains that the Mawangdui *I Ching* is almost a thousand years older than the standard version, and that its 'errors' made sense to the nobles of Changsha. Maybe these poor souls just didn't know any better, but the oracle seems to have satisfied them. Is such a thing as a wrong *I Ching* possible? If you divine a hexagram, is the correct answer to be found in the standard or the Mawangdui text? Worse yet, are any of the answers in error? Such troubles only exercise the minds of those who seek their oracle in an exterior form and have problems with keeping two concepts in the mind at the same time.

If you have any experience with other forms of divination, such as the tarot or the runes, you will be quite comfortable with a single symbol that possesses several highly diverse meanings. In fact, a divination system improves when it provides multiple interpretations. If you consult your deep mind, instead of a book, you will find the answer that suits you. This crucial step, however, requires an almost playful attitude. Instead of searching for the true answer, you could focus on an answer that reveals something new.

A divination is not worth much if it merely confirms what you assumed anyway. If it makes you *think differently* you may gain valuable insights from assuming unusual points of view. One does not need a 'true' oracle for this purpose. It suffices to change the perspective, or to interpret the familiar in a novel form. In this sense I hope that the information-overload of this essay suffices to stimulate your mind in creative and unexpected ways.

It may be worth considering that to the owner of the tomb library of Mawangdui the *I Ching* was a more fluid and subtle source of advice than to many literally minded people. Was the original *I Ching* read silently, spoken or recited aloud? Spoken Chinese carries many layers of meaning, and the characters of the text may have given way to multiple interpretations as soon as the answer was uttered. It might even be hypothesized that there was no such thing as an original written *I Ching*. The early diviners used to memorize their oracles in some poetic or songlike form, as can be observed in several oracular systems, then the original *I Ching* had lots of meanings at once. It lost them as soon as it was committed to writing but regained them by being spoken once more.

The basic use of words in Taoism is to suggest meaning. Words need not be precise, it is more useful when they stimulate. The same goes for the use of signs, such as the trigrams and many others. Symbols should not be precise if they are to make sense in divination. If the eight trigrams are to provide you with lots of answers for all conceivable situations, they have to be loose enough to offer your deep mind freedom of choice. That this is entirely in keeping with early Chinese philosophy appears in the *I Ching* commentaries of Wang Bi (226-249 CE), (translated after Hertzer) :

'*Symbols serve to express ideas. Words serve to explain symbols. (. . .) Thus, the aim of words is to explain the symbols, but as soon as the symbols are understood, the words may be forgotten. The aim of the symbols is to preserve the ideas, but as soon as the ideas are grasped, the symbols may be forgotten.*'

Can you imagine what is hidden behind the ideas?

2 Simplicity Itself

An essay on the art of Taoist Meditation

Perhaps you are one of those adventurous souls who would like to learn about a topic that is harder to write about than to practice. Maybe you already have some knowledge of that most paradoxical world-view cultivated by the early Taoists and ask yourself just what is the actual meditation that those adepts developed in order to refine the awareness of the Tao. This is not quite an easy topic, as the practises of the early Taoist sages, though of a relatively simple nature when compared with other oriental disciplines, underwent a lot of changes over the millennia. Also, these authors were not really interested in giving simple instructions. In their eyes, meditative practises were priceless treasures that should not be wasted on vulgar folk or people greedy for instant results. As a result, much of the terminology that they favoured is deliberately obscure and sometimes even misleading. Playing with words and double or triple meanings were part of what constituted good literary style, and obviously such refinements cannot be translated into Western languages. More complicated yet, a good many essentials of meditative practise belong to a realm of awareness that cannot be framed in ordinary language. As you can see, we're in for a lot of fun. It can be helpful to approach the study of this subject with a healthy doses of ignorance. This is one of my favourite strategies when working with cryptic writings that supposedly come from some period of mythical prehistory. When you recognize your ignorance you get a chance to learn something new. You are humbly requested not to trust my interpretations of this subject but to cultivate an open mind and to test the theory by putting it to practise.

The Tao is not a topic for idle philosophical debate. It's not even suited for essays. Whatever you or I may put into words is not the Tao itself but a vague approximation. To understand Tao you are invited to experience it. This may be easier said than done, but once you set out and actually do it, you may find that the doing is a lot easier than the saying.

In the beginning

It might help to start our exploration right at the beginning, in the earliest stage of Taoism. Popular belief ascribes the invention of Taoism to the almost legendary figure of the Yellow Emperor Huang Ti (Huangdi) and to the equally obscure sage Lao Tsu (Laozi). This sage, if we can trust the myths, was born in 604 BCE out of the left armpit of his mother. You may observe that this is not exactly the usual way of making one's entry into the world, but then, the dear lady had been pregnant with him for 72 years and was mightily relieved to be rid of him, no matter how.

The dear babe came to the world of yellow earth with long, white hair and a trailing beard. His real name is unknown to us but later traditions named him Li (or Lao) Tan. The common name Lao Tsu is not a proper name but more like an affectionate nickname meaning 'Old Sage', or Old Boy if you like. The latter may be more accurate as Lao Tsu aimed at remaining young and succeeded remarkably. Legend has it that he wrote 80 books on practical magic, none of which has survived. Another legend claims that Lao Tsu worked as a historian in the state archive of the Chou. Eventually Chou became corrupt. The old sage foresaw the threatening downfall of the state, packed his scant belongings and left. When he felt the time of his death approaching, he decided to leave the middle kingdom. Riding on a black water buffalo, he made his way to the west (i.e. the direction of sunset, hence death) but when he came to the Han Ku pass, Yin Hi (or Hsi), the guardian on duty stopped the venerable saint and asked him not to leave the world before he had put down the quintessence of his teachings in yet another book.

The result was the famous *Tao Te Ching*, a remarkable work in 81 chapters, that became something like the manifesto of the Taoist movement. It also turned Yin Hi into an immortal, which goes to show that reading books can be dangerous and ought to be avoided if possible.

Unlike the other (legendary) works of the old master, the *Tao Te Ching* appears as an almost mystical text. It is not directly concerned with the practise of magic or meditation but proposes a sublime philosophy that functions on many layers of meaning. So much for the legendary account. In more prosaic reality, historians have long decided that the *Tao Te Ching* was not composed in the sixth but the fourth or even third century BCE, and that the popular Lao Tsu, well known from shrines in Chinese restaurants all over the world, never existed at all. This is a bit like the scholarly debate whether Shakespeare really lived - a lot of academics who can't write get together to decide that an author who could did not exist. Sinologists have become extremely shy about admitting that a person of whom we only know the pseudonym actually lived, a question that would have seemed remarkably absurd to most Taoists and to Lao Tsu himself. Be that as it may, there is such a book as the *Tao Te Ching*, and regardless who wrote it, the work has been a popular manual of philosophy and mysticism ever since. In searching for the roots of Taoist meditation, the first question is what awareness the wisdom of the text is supposed to cultivate. At the first glance, the *Tao Te Ching* is not a book that seems entirely practical. This impression may be deceptive.

One of the pioneers of mind exploration, Tim Leary, used the texts of the good book like a hypnotic suggestion. He had the chapters read to people who were tripping on acid, and found all sorts of amazing insights dawning in their minds. This was a reinvention of an old

Lao Tsu riding the black buffalo

magickal technique that aims at changing consciousness by listening. Story-telling partakes of this magick, and so do all rituals of recitation. The use of acid was his own little addition, and one that was not really required. If you listen to anything as contents free and structure stimulating as the *Tao Te Ching* with full awareness, changes in your mind and understanding are bound to happen. The acid just made things easier - but any good trance state induced by hypnotic suggestion would do the job quite as well, and possibly with more elegance.

The Lao Tsu of Chinese folk belief was not just a mythical human but soon acquired the status of a deity. This made his work a bit of holy writ and implied that people could pray to him and ask him for all sorts of help and support. Whether he would have appreciated this development remains uncertain - after all, the *Tao Te Ching* puts very little emphasis on divine beings and is definitely not a religious work. Just for fun's sake, the early Taoists declared that Lao Tsu's final journey to the west meant that he was reborn as the Buddha in India. This tale did a lot to annoy Buddhists.

Though the *Tao Te Ching* is not a large book it requires study and insight to fathom its more subtle meanings. For our present purpose it suffices to take a look at the more meditative passages of the *Tao Te Ching*. As an inspiring work I can't recommend it too highly. In this I'm not alone.

Aleister Crowley (1875-1947) was highly enchanted by the work and produced his own translation in 1918ev, mainly by the simple expedient of rearranging the classic translation of James Legge (1891). While this can hardly be called a translation, the result does make sense. Crowley, though he did not speak much Chinese, had the great advantage that he knew what he was talking about. Unlike most scholars he was well acquainted with the art of meditation and magick and consequently he did not get caught by questions relating to linguistic complications. While this does not sound like an overly trustworthy approach to a difficult ancient text, it is certainly in keeping with the spirit of Taoism. There are plenty of Chinese authors who pointed out that the easiest way to misunderstand the *Tao Te*

Ching is to take it literally.

Austin Spare was similarly fascinated. His literary works, starting quite early, contain many indirect references to Taoism and paraphrases of Lao Tsu's aphorisms. In the 'Prayer of Adoration' (see *The Witches' Sabbath*, Fulgur 1992), he even invoked:

> '*Thou lambent spirit of Erh! Thou hast kindled the sacred fire from dead ashes, so my torch lightens all darknesses.*'

Gavin Semple told me that the name Erh, also spelled as Er or simply R was a name of Lao Tsu. You can find this odd bit of information in several translations of the *Tao Te Ching*, such as the versions of James Legge (1891) and Dr. Paul Carus (1898) which contains the statement: *His family was the Li gentry (Li meaning plum). His proper name was Er (Ear), his posthumous title Po-Yang (Prince Positive), his appellation Tan (Long-Lobed)*. These were the translations that Austin Spare was familiar with. Neither of them is very authoritative nowadays (the *Prince Positive* is not the sort of term that modern sinologists would get away with) but they sufficed to deeply influence Spare's philosophy. In fact Spare came closer to an understanding of the Tao than could be claimed of Legge. Gavin Semple proposed that:

> '*In the context of the conjuration in Witches Sabbath, Li Erh is addressed as the personification of the Neither-Neither/Kia; Spare uses him as a "type", hence, "Thou Emissary of Neither-Neither..."- a sort of Prophet of the Voidness.*'

This makes the Old Boy a patron saint of one of the most fascinating modern magical systems.

Lao Tsu might have been surprised to be invoked as a *lambent spirit*, especially after looking up the many meanings the word *lambent* can have. But let us turn from the historical person (who never really existed, as Lao Tsu's spirit assures me) to the question of how he came to have so many brilliant insights. People are not born as sages, usually they have to do something to develop the required consciousness.

Where do we find meditation in the *Tao Te Ching*? First of all, we could take a look at the oldest known version of the text. The standard version that you can find in plenty of translations goes back to the philosopher Wang Bi, who composed his commentary in the third century CE, i.e. circa six or seven centuries after the composition of the original. Wang Bi's version used to be the oldest complete version of the text. However there were a couple of older fragments around. Then came the discovery of the Mawangdui grave library which contained two different versions of the text, both of them more or less complete (but tattered) and dating from 168 BCE. While most of the words of Wang Bi's version turned out to be remarkably accurate, there are a couple of differences well worth considering.

As you probably know, the book consists of two parts. The first deals with the Tao (Dao), an abstract concept that has been translated as the way, development, process, method, meaning or even speaking. None of these meanings is sufficient to express the full depths of the term and each of them misleads when considered on its own. Lao Tsu, whoever he was, enjoyed to play with the many meanings of the term but sadly this does not make it into other languages. As chapter 45 (chapter 1 of the standard version) tells us,

> '*One Tao - can it be called Tao it is not the permanent Tao.*'

Alternatively, this line could be given as

> '*The way that can be walked is not the permanent way*'

or

> '*The method that can be called method is not the permanent method.*'

Thus, even the most simple definition of the word Tao contains a wide scope of possible meanings. Whatever the old sage intended, it was not confined to a single interpretation. The original idea of the Tao is just too inclusive (or should we call it elusive?) to be limited by words.

The second part is dedicated to the cultivation of the Te (De), which can be translated as virtue, power, and especially magical power. As a cheerful oversimplification one might claim that the Tao describes the universal flow of development and change while the Te is the force that allows the adept to go with the flow of the Tao. This is a lie, as any sinologist could tell you, but for the time being it will do. If you want a better definition you can easily find it in the writings of Lao Tsu himself. Do yourself a favour and read them, if possible in several translations.

Now the first surprise in the Mawangdui texts is that they reverse the accustomed order, and begin the work with the section dealing with the Te. Chapter 1 of the Mawangdui versions corresponds with chapter 38 of the standard text. This means that the original title of the book ought to be the *Te Tao Ching*, but you can ignore this, as nobody would understand what you are talking about anyway. What is more important is that the understanding of the Tao begins after the virtue, or magical energy has been cultivated. This is already a practical insight. Tao is not a wishy washy concept that one is supposed to swallow for the sake of faith and gullibility but an experience arising naturally out of the cultivation of magical power. In essence, one is not supposed to believe in the Tao but to experience it. The way to come to this experience is refinement of the mind, a steady process of re-attaining simplicity and the original nature of selfhood. All through Chinese literature, the term 'to cultivate the Tao' is used for this meditational practise.

Essentials of Taoism

Let us now take a look at the advise the *Tao Te Ching* offers for practicing mind explorers. At the first glance, practical advise is not very obvious in the text. Where the standard version is addressed at a reader who is described as a saint or a sage, the Mawangdui texts are more political and identify the saint with the ruler. Therefore, much of the material is aimed at the correct way of ruling the people. But

Taoist thought is full of subtlety and multiple meanings. The way of governing a country corresponds with the way the sage governs body and mind, so that a political metaphor can be interpreted as an instruction in the art of refining oneself. Essentially this is done by Not-Doing (wu wei), by non-interference and by allowing things to develop naturally (ziran). Good regents do not interfere, good superiors do not meddle, and the conscious mind does not tell the body how to do its job.

However the not-doing of Taoism is not quite as passive as it seems. As the *Spring and Autumn Annals of Lü Bu We* keep repeating, the regent's function is not to interfere in the task of ruling the country. After all, the regent, no matter how clever he is, cannot understand everything. The brain does not tell the stomach how to digest food, as the stomach knows more about this job than the brain ever will. A good regent knows that if he interferes, no matter how good his intentions, things will certainly be upset. A wise ruler searches for competent ministers and honours them. Then the ministers do all the specialist jobs that the regent can't, and every one is happy. In a similar fashion the saintly king of the *Tao Te Ching* remains humble, lonely and ignorant. He merely produces an atmosphere or a setting that allows the most competent experts to fulfill their specialist function with great ease and harmony.

Applied to the practise of meditation, the basic idea is that you create auspicious conditions. You do not attempt to control things or to manipulate them. Instead, you allow yourself to return to such a state of silence and simplicity that the desired result, union with the flow of the Tao, occurs naturally and without effort. This concept is a long way from the complicated techniques that are favoured by Indian Yogis or the result-orientation cultivated by so many Western systems of attainment. Now the usual reaction to such an art of simplicity is to ask 'but what shall I do?' This is a good but misleading question, as most of the doing is not-doing and all the results occur naturally when one is not striving to achieve them. Luckily, Lao Tsu was kind enough to offer a bit of advice from time to time. The first essential of Taoist meditation is to return to the origin, to the nameless state of natural simplicity. The old sage was of the opinion that the outer world is something of a trap for attention. When your awareness is tied to the ten thousand things that happen around you, it is unlikely that your mind will become empty and silent enough to realize the nameless, all embracing Tao. Thus, one of the first aims of the sage is to draw attention inwards, i.e. to dissociate the awareness of the outer world.

In several chapters of the *Tao Te Ching* this process is given.

'To close the apertures, to shut the gates, to reduce brilliance, to level the dust, to blunt the sharp, to unravel the tangles : this is called the hidden (dark) unity.'

These lines appear in chapters 19 (56) and 48 (4) of the Mawangdui texts. Chapter 15 (52) adds:

'Close the apertures, shut the gates, remain unburdened by the end of the body. Open the apertures, involve yourself in activity, remain unsaved from the end of the body.'

These lines contain several useful suggestions. The gates, orifices or apertures are the means by which humans interact with and sense the world. To close them is to withdraw inwards, and to return to the original unity. The saint withdraws from the world by returning attention to its source, the way to the Tao is a backwards path. Reducing brilliance can be a way of making visual imagination less fascinating. To keep the dust level means not to stir it: this could refer to the Taoist way of meditative breathing. All of the three major sensory systems are reversed:

'What one gazes at and does not see: it is called minute. What one listens for and does not hear: it is called silent. What one gropes for and does not grasp: it is called smooth. Ultimately, these three cannot be measured. Merge them and they become one.' Chapter 58 (14).

These lines, while seeming to be of a philosophical nature, can also be seen as a useful instruction. In each sense a sensation that cannot be perceived is sought and cultivated. One does not only seek silence, for instance, but actively listens for it. This is not the silence that is merely the absence of sound but the primal matrix out of which sound takes its shape. Such silence exists no matter how loud it seems to be around you. It can be found, or if you like, it can be made. When you withdraw your attention from sound it appears naturally. Likewise, to see what is too small to be seen and to hold what is too smooth or slippery to be grasped is a way of attaining that which lies beyond, or even before the senses. If you wish to cultivate inner silence, as is the aim of many systems of attainment, one way to do so is to listen to silence, to your own silence, as if it were something you could hear. Can you see the invisible, and can you feel the non-existant? Can you perceive or imagine an impossible sensation?

> *'To attain vacuity is the ultimate. To keep silence is control. The ten thousand things happen one after the other: observe wither they develop. The things of the world consist of diversity; they all return to their roots. This is called silence.'* - 60 (16)

As you will notice, the way of the Tao is a way of becoming evermore simple until you are entirely absent. If you confuse this with nihilism you are missing something vital. What remains after you are gone? Any answer to this question may be misleading. How about finding out? When we examine the teachings of Lao Tsu, we can discern the fundamental principles of Taoist practise in them. Many of them are not quite specified, but as you will realize when we take a look at the later Taoists, they are already present in embryonic form.

Immortality

Let me introduce you to the roots of the doctrine of 'immortality'. There will be more on this topic in the next chapter but it may help if the matter is already mentioned here. The common expression 'Immortal' is a mistranslation of an essential Taoist concept. There are plenty of immortal sages in Taoist myth, and immortality is often called the primary aim of Taoist practice. Well, the very idea of immortality is a misunderstanding. Chinese thought does not allow for anything to exist forever, and the notion that people could attain this state is neither likely nor especially desirable. To live forever is only a pleasant thought for those who are not too good at thinking. The famed immortals of Taoism are usually people who have transcended the limits of the ego and the world it believes in. As long as an ego remains immortality is impossible, and without an ego, there is nobody left to experience immortality.

It says a lot that in the legends the so called immortals occasionally happen to die. This does not seem to affect them much, as after dying they tend to leave the world of humans, and return to spiritual realms and otherworldly paradises where they can enjoy drinking and singing with their associates until the time for re-manifestation or rebirth comes again. In this model, it is not the body but the consciousness that is immortal, and even this is subject to change and transformation. The consciousness, however, is not the same thing as the personality. More precisely, it is no thing at all.

Take another look at the injunction that one should close the gates and doors of the body. These lines have been interpreted as a formula to preserve health by conserving the Ch'i energy, the vital force of life. Many Taoists thought that they could extend the length of their lifetimes by making sure that no vital energy is lost, and this idea, once developed, led to a number of obsessive practices that were supposed to close and seal the body. A school of thought developed that sought to avoid loss of Ch'i . As its adepts believed, Ch'i is lost in several ways. To ejaculate, for instance, was to lose a lot of vitality, and consequently, orgasms of the usual sort were strictly to be avoided. Pissing was thought to be dangerous, too, but luckily the stimulation of certain energy meridians in the body could ensure that not too much Ch'i was lost. Sweating was also wasteful, and some of the totally obsessed feared to eat onions and beans as farting was a sure way of reducing ones life expectation. Of course such an extreme attitude is not much in tune with the 'go with the flow' philosophy of Lao Tsu. His writings make it clear that a striving for longevity for its own sake has nothing in common with the way of the sages, who saw birth and death as natural and inevitable events. Chuang Tsu, commenting on the death of Lao Tsu, wrote:

'The Master came because it was time. He left because he followed the natural flow.'

The quest for immortality, on the other hand, was favoured by people who desperately clung to life, and the corpses of the western Han period supply charming examples. In this period the high ranking aristocrats used to be buried in suits made out of jade pieces that were carefully sewn together in order to enclose the entire body. The oldest complete set was found in a tomb in Hebei. It dates around 113 BCE. Jade was thought to make the body incorruptible and the spirit immortal. To make really sure that not one bit of energy might escape, all apertures of the body were closed with jade plugs. The only hole in such jade costumes was at the very top of the head, allowing the heavenly soul (hun) to escape while the soul of the body (po) remained trapped by the jade plugs. This was supposed to prevent decay. Consequently, those nobles made lively corpses, not that this did them any good. This sort of belief may have developed out of Lao Tsu's writings, but we shouldn't blame him for it.

Meditation and story telling

But let us return to the topic of meditation. Another early author who influenced the development of Taoism is the enigmatic Chuang Tsu (Zhuangzi). While Lao Tsu described the flow of the Tao in verse, Chuang Tsu was an expert story teller. If you have experience with hypnotherapy you may be aware that stories do have a tendency to stimulate transformations in the deep mind. Normal speech may easily be forgotten but stories are easily remembered. More so, when a story is enigmatic, the deep mind will insist of making sense of it, if need be by inventing a meaning for the tale. Stories are psycho-active material, and this is the main reason why I bother you with weird tales of all descriptions.

Such stories may seem silly but they stimulate the deep mind. We know even less about Chuang Tsu than about Lao Tsu. His work was supposedly written in the third century BCE. It contains many references to Lao Tsu, who was described as a contemporary of Kung Tsu (Confucius), but how far this tale accords with historical reality is rather hard to decide. As I'm sure that you will read Chuang Tsu's works anyway, I'll just comment on a few items on meditation that lurk here and there in his tales. You may recall the expression 'fasting the heart', a term for a meditative practice already alluded to in the essay on the *I Ching*. In Chuang Tsu's writings, the expression is put into the mouth of Kung Tsu (he made Kung Tsu say a lot of things that are highly unlike the material that the historic Kung Tsu actually preached about). The passage is a bit difficult, I follow the translation by M. Buber.

' *"Cultivate unity"* answered Khung Tse *"You do not listen with the ears but with the mind; not with the mind but with the soul. But let the hearing stop at the ears. Let the activity of the mind stop with itself. Then your soul will be an independent being that responds to the things with the not-doing of undivided unity. Such an independent being alone can be the dwelling place of the Tao. And this state of release is the fasting of the heart."* '

We could compare this activity with dissociation. To understand it fully, keep in mind that the term 'heart' has a different meaning in Chinese thought than in European Philosophy. In Europe, the heart was the seat of emotion but in China the heart was a metaphor for such concepts as mind, attention or thought. Thus, the primary aim of this meditation is to empty the mind and to return to a state of voidness and simplicity that allows the Tao to manifest spontaneously. There are several Taoist meditations that aim at fasting the heart, some of them complicated and technical, some of them so simple that they cannot be described, but they all aim at the same consciousness, which is also no consciousness, and cannot be properly defined anyway. Another element of meditation is stillness. Just as thought is voided and the inner voice brought to silence, the body is allowed to calm down and to rest. We find the first hints of this idea in the *I Ching*, in the sign 'Keeping Still, Mountain' which is closely connected with meditation, as well as gaining access to the realm of the spirits through the gate of life.

Speaking of the qualities of the sage-rulers, Chuang Tsu tells us:

'If he can refrain from damaging his inner balance and from exhausting his senses, if he is as motionless as a corpse while his dragon power manifests everywhere, in deep silence while his thundering voice sounds, all the forces of heaven will follow the motion of his will and through the gentle influence of not doing all things thrive and come to ripeness. What leisure would he have to govern the world?'

The corpse

The idea of being as motionless as a corpse might be worth considering here. As you will know, there are plenty of mystical and shamanic systems that make use of a trance in which the practitioner experiences her or his own death, preferably repeatedly. A good example can be found in the Tibetan *Chöd* (to cut) rituals and in the countless Eurasian shamanic traditions. Here, the aspiring shaman fully experiences what it is like to die. Then the corpse becomes a sacrificial offering to the gods and spirits who devour it at leisure. In a later stage of the rite the shaman is reassembled by the gods and spirits, who, having devoured her/him, have become allies and friends. The bones are usually laid out and clothed with fresh flesh, and when the shaman comes out of the trance s/he is a new being, reborn, and fully initiated.

Keep in mind that the gods and spirits who perform this rite of transformation are not nice. Many of them are the most horrible entities the shaman can imagine, demons of disease and horror who are deliberately sought in dangerous and desolate places. There are of course plenty of local variations to this trance ritual. Siberian shamans, for example, are often reassembled in a somewhat crude fashion. The spirits of disease, who have devoured the corpse, throw up the digested body. They re-arrange the bones and bind them with iron wire. They put the new shaman together and the place her/him in a nest on the world tree where s/he can grow up and learn the secrets of the trade.

In the Tibetan version, the new body of the Chödpa is crafted out of rainbow radiance. While most of the Siberian shamans only undergo this willed death and rebirth a few times, the Chödpas make it a regular ritual and believe that it actually stimulates health. This is a notion I very much agree with. Similar rituals can be found in the death and resurrection ritual of Christian Rosenkreuz or in Austin Spare's Death Posture trances. But let us return to the Taoists. It is entirely possible that the comparison of the unmoving adept with a corpse actually hints at an identification with a corpse, and this is certainly one of the easiest and most efficient ways of voiding the heart and everything else. Another passage of Chuang Tsu's writings, (after Buber) elaborates this theme.

> '*Tse-Khi from Nan-Kuo sat leaning over his table. He gazed at the sky, his breath was deep and soft and he seemed withdrawn as if his body and soul had parted. Yen-Cheng Tse-Yü, who was standing before him, called: "What is happening within you, that your body becomes like a dry tree and your mind like dead ashes? Verily, the man who is leaning over this table is not the one that he used to be." Tse-Khi replied: "You ask for good reason. Today, I have buried myself. Can you understand?"* '

However having died, Tse-Khi was able to experience the harmony and music of heaven itself and to come back with a remarkable tale.

In these lines we encounter a common concept of Taoism. This is the law of reversal, which postulates that things that reach their extreme form revert into their opposites. Thus the *Tao Te Ching*, chapter 13 (50) states that '*to go out into life is to enter into death.*' If this formula is reversed, a journey into death equals a return to life. This comes close to the daily practise of the Chödpas. One might imagine that a daily trance that elaborates dying might have a bad effect on health and vitality. On the contrary the Chödpas were thought to be so resistant against disease and death that the funeral rites were left to them. They were the ones who could dare to cut up the corpse into pieces and feed it to the vultures without fear of infection by plague or disease. Somehow their close alliance with the spirits of destruction supplied them with better than average health and often a wild sense of humour as well.

Lieh Tsu (Liezi), who lived before Chuang Tsu, commented:

'*Life that arises out of death is joy.*'

He also informed us that unless things reach their extremes, they do not revert into their opposites. This may give you a clue why the chödpas or their shamanic colleagues do not just imagine a humble death but make the visualization and the self-offering as horrible and dramatic an event as possible.

Shamanism

In this place it might be worth mentioning that Taoism has a lot in common with shamanism. Most scholars of the Western world ignore this connection, and pretend that the writings of Lao Tsu and Chuang Tsu are of a purely mystical quality that has nothing to do with spirits and deities, let alone rituals and ceremonies. I have often read commentaries claiming that the supposedly pure Taoism of the early times was later distorted by superstitious rituals, banishings, sacrifices and public ceremonies, and that these practices show a tainting of the original form with folkloristic sorceries. Such an interpretation is only possible when one sees magick as a stupid superstition. In

Chuang Tsu and the Butterfly

China, 'philosophical' Taoism was always closely related to ceremonial rituals. It is an interesting detail that chapter 23 (60) of the *Tao Te Ching* advises the sage to order the places in the world according to the Tao, so that the spirits do not work evil or injure the population. Under these conditions neither the spirits nor the sage will harm the people. When two do not harm each other (the spirits and the sage) the magical power (Te) is transmitted and returns to the sage. This is good evidence for the belief that the sage actually derives magical power from the spirits. These lines are clearer in the Mawangdui version than in the standard text. They are not far from the Siberian idea that the shaman derives the power to heal from her/his allies, who are the very spirits responsible for the disease in the first place.

And what of the charming tale of Chuang Tsu, who found a skull and used it as his pillow in order to communicate with the spirit it used to house? This might be explained as an allegory, but essentially it comes pretty close to necromancy. Several passages in Chuang Tsu's works can be interpreted as oblique references to shamanism. Best known is the episode of the butterfly dream. Chuang Tsu slept and dreamed that he was a butterfly. Happily he flew from blossom to blossom. Then evening came and the butterfly settled down for the night. It fell asleep and dreamed that it was the Philosopher Chuang Tsu. Recovering from this startling transformation, the sage wondered who he really was, a butterfly dreaming a human dream or a man dreaming a butterfly dream. If you take this tale for a mind game or a fable you are missing something. Perhaps the sage invented an allegory, but possibly this allegory is a reflection of a trance experience. Could it be that Chuang Tsu transformed into an animal spirit? A butterfly would be a magnificent expression of the hidden side of his nature, and the fact that the butterfly dream was as real as the human dream says a lot about the sages power to associate fully with it. The next time you see a butterfly fluttering between the flowers at the wayside, take a close look and consider how it finds its way. What seems like an erratic path may well follow a hidden plan. The early Taoists thought highly of magick, but they especially praised the

Fire flares up, water flows down, the way of heaven is round.

variety that is inconspicuous. Lieh Tsu even remarked:

> *'The competent magician uses his mysterious powers secretly, his deeds resemble those of ordinary people.'*

These lines, written around 300 BCE and before the writings of Chuang Tsu, show that magic was not a late deviation of the Taoists but fully cultivated right at the beginning of the movement. There is a lot of magic in ancient Taoism that is rarely recognized as it moves in subtle ways.

Chuang Tsu was helpful enough to give a few more hints on the requirements of this art. Let me quote from Gia-Fu Feng's translation:

> *'Yen Hui said, "I am not attached to the body and I give up any idea of knowing. By freeing myself from the body and mind, I become one with the infinite. This is what I mean by sitting and forgetting."'*

Or consider these enigmatic lines:

> *'Wander where there is no path. Be all that heaven gave you, but act as though you have received nothing. Be empty, that is all. The mind of a perfect man is like a mirror. It grasps nothing. It expects nothing. It reflects but does not hold. Therefore, the perfect man can act without effort.'*

Again, these ideas have their parallels in the writings of Lao Tsu. Chapter 54 (10) states:

> *'When you nourish the soul and embrace unity, can you keep wholeness? When you concentrate Ch'i and attain softness, can you be like a child? When you purify and clean the dark mirror, can you become stainless?'*

In passages like these, the effects of meditation are hinted at. Luckily, they are not fully defined, giving us the freedom to develop as it suits our nature. Sadly, they are a bit too abstract to make most people happy, and this goes especially for modern Magicians, who tend to get things done by going out and doing them. The early Taoist authors were seldom really definite in their instructions, but this attitude changed in later periods.

So far, the fundamental ideas in meditation can be summed up as follows. Keep the body still. Withdraw attention from the senses. Introvert attention. Allow your mind to calm down. Gradually, become empty and void. Forget your intentions and yourself, and Tao may manifest on its own accord. This is not achieved by doing and effort but happens naturally.

In the works attributed to Huai Nan Tsu (Huainanzi), who died in 122BCE, the earlier ideas are further elaborated. Not in the magnificent poetic metaphors of Chuang Tsu but in a simple and down to earth manner that is just as true and misleading. The sages, so Huai Nan Tsu wrote, return to the beginning of the ten thousand things, i.e. to the Hun Tun. They see the formless and hear the inaudible. Their perception is clear. Their eyes see, but are not used for seeing. Their ears hear, but are not used for listening. Their mind is wide, but is not used for thinking. They are free from obsessive desires, their energy is calm and contained and their mood is relaxed and joyous.

Joy is one of the key elements of all practice. It may be worth considering that in this early stage of Taoist literature the desires are not as fully condemned as in later periods, when the influence of Buddhist philosophy made desire in itself a great evil and a form of bondage to suffering. In the Mawangdui versions of the *Tao Te Ching* you can find the lines (Chapter 45 (1)):

'*Always without desire, to see the subtle; always with desire, to see what is required.*'

Later interpreters put a stop to this ambiguous attitude. The standard version of them certainly looks different. The Taoist sage was believed to be without any sort of desire and joy was considered a threat to the tranquillity the sage was supposed to cultivate. That this is evidently nonsense can be realized by the most superficial acquaintance with the famous *Eight Immortals*. Take a look at their images and pictures: they are usually shown laughing. The point is that any prohibition does not accord with the free flow of the Tao. To make desires undesirable is to desire to be without desires. People who persist in this can get themselves into interesting states. Instead of being trapped in this fascinating double-bind, the early Taoist refuses to insist. Obviously it takes greater skill to cope with desires than to prohibit them, but then, a prohibition can be a worse form of bondage than the original desire itself.

Sacred spaces

While the instructions of the early sages may be of use to some, there are lots of people who require more technical help. Consequently, the different schools of Taoism developed a number of techniques to make things easier. These techniques were basically conveniences. Some of them made use of visualization, of mantrams, mudras, or ceremony. Others involved days of purification, fasting, isolation or obscure drugs and medicines. An incredible scope of bizarre methods were developed to suit the various needs of students, and it would far exceed the size of this essay to list even half of them.

With the development of these methods came an ever greater complication. People began to think that some techniques are better than others, and forgot that the ultimate aim of all technique is to do without it. Thus, a formidable growth of secret methods was stimulated, and those who fell prey to their fascination soon forgot that the experience of the Tao depends on simplicity and voidness. Not that it is especially easy to cultivate a voidness that is not void but contains everything while being nothing and that defies description anyway. If this makes sense to you I probably did not phrase it properly.

The techniques of Taoist meditation were originally developed to help those students who found simplicity too simple (or was that difficult?). Among the earliest are attention of energy centers within body and breathing. Lets take a look at occult anatomy. Like the Hindu

Yogis, the Taoists believed (or hypothesized) a number of hidden energy centers within the body. Some of them are like the chakras known from Yoga, with the difference that Chinese lore knows more of them, describes them with different metaphors. Where the Yogis imagine the chakras as wheels or lotus flowers the Taoists preferred to see (or imagine) them as hollow places, ovens and furnaces, as rooms, halls, cauldrons and vessels.

There are several ways in which these sacred spaces are put to meditative use. The simplest of them is to allow awareness to dwell on one of these spots. This is called focusing attention on a hollow. There are plenty of them around, and literature is not at all congruent when it comes to choosing the proper one. To list just a few of them, you can find the upper field within your head, the middle field in your torso between heart and navel and the lower cinnabar field, the dragons castle in the depth of the ocean, in the lower belly a bit below the navel. The last is one of the best known as it is so important in the martial arts.

Other spaces are in the genitals, the perineum, the base of the spine, on the spine at the height of the lower and middle field, between the shoulders, in the neck, in the back of the head, on top of the head, between the eyebrows, between the eyes, the tip of the nose, the roof of your mouth, the tip of the tongue, the throat, the breastbone, the hands, feet, heels, the inner organs plus some sites that exist outside of the body. This list is not complete nor does it have to be.

Basically, there are lots of power places in the body and some authors got so deeply involved in their study that they sought to identify their exact location to the half inch. To make things worse, there are several flowery terms for each center, and as often as not, such terms were not only deliberately obscure but also not in agreement with the writings of other researchers. While the methods of inner alchemy, which were aimed at attaining enlightenment through the refinement of these spaces, got increasingly complicated over the centuries, there was also a more simple approach. This school of thought postulated that those people who find it hard to empty the mind and attain Tao without technique may eventually benefit by keeping the mind steady on one of these centers. The center was seen as a guiding idea, a means of calming thought and focusing attention. It was not necessarily sacred but simply useful. Thus, a number of authors proposed that one should focus attention on one of the vessels. Again, this proposal came in two forms. A lot of authors recommended that their own favourite was the perfect focus, and some of them were obsessive enough to define the exact location of the vessel. Others merely noted that some spaces gave easier results than others, and claimed that insistence on exact locations leads to diseases. In their opinion, a general awareness of the space was much preferable to a precise spot. Some went beyond this and recalled that any awareness of a sacred space was merely a convenience. If you focus awareness on your lower cinnabar field, for instance, this can be a useful means of steadying attention and refining breath. Should you happen to forget this place from time to time this is a good sign, as union with the Tao does not occur when people strain their minds with obsessive concentration. Any form of insistence is a form of rigidity and thus against the flow of the Tao. The later alchemists expressed this point when they stated that the architect uses angles and measures to check if the building develops properly. He does not stare at them all the time.

'The way of heaven'

Yet another school of thought proposed a complicated visualization. Attention, visualized as a tiny golden serpent, was to move from space to space in the body. This comes close to the Hindu concept of the Kundalini serpent/deity. Unlike the Kundalini, however, the Taoist serpent does not go up and down the spine in a vertical line. Chinese occult anatomy is not as concerned with up and down as the Hindu model. The serpent moves from the perineum upwards, makes its way through a couple of passes along the spine, goes up the back of the head and reaches the crown of the skull. So far the journey is much like the

Yoga model. Then it transforms and moves downwards in the form of an elixir. This is sometimes achieved by mingling it with the spittle. You could imagine that the elixir moves along the front of your face, passes between your eyes, and collects in the mouth.

Gritting the teeth and churning the tongue produces a lot of saliva. Some adepts improved on this by drawing sigils on the roof of the mouth with the tongue, or by visualizing all sorts of coloured vapors. When the saliva has become properly charged it is swallowed. Thereby, the attention/elixir moves down again, but not along the spine but through the throat, the stomach, past the navel, the lower cinnabar field, the genitals and back to the perineum.

As you can see, this journey is a circuit and attention follows an ovoid path around body. Usually, around thirteen sacred spaces are passed along the way, but of course there are quite a few differences in the details when you examine the accounts of various authors. In some systems the saliva swallowing is emphasized, in others it is completely absent and the whole operation takes place entirely in the imagination. What I like best about this method is the fact that the self is refined while the energy/awareness goes round and round. This alchemical procedure is practiced continuously, not only during meditation but in daily life. An early reference to this technique may be Lü Bu We's adage:

'The force of life ascends and descends, contained in a round circuit, without blockage or barrier. Thus is is said: "the way of heaven is round."'

You can find good accounts of it in the work of Chang Bo Tuan (Zhang Boduan) who lived 983 to 1082 and in the two remarkable texts that Richard Wilhelm published in *The Secret of the Golden Flower*. These are not exactly easy reading but can be comprehended eventually, provided one ignores the totally misleading commentaries that C.G.Jung supplied to the translation. The attempt to explain the two souls of Chinese belief (hun and po) with the highly questionable concepts of Anima and Animus could have been done without, but a detailed treatment of this issue would be a bit too extensive for this essay.

The roots of this alchemical refinement can be found in the writings attributed to Lü Tung Pin (Lü Dongbin or Lü Yan) who lived sometime after 600 CE and is nowadays known as one of the most popular immortals. You can recognize his figure in numerous Chinese shrines by the sword and the fly whisk he is carrying. His literary work gives a lot of detailed advice regarding the refinement of vital essence, Ch'i energy, and the primal consciousness. It is not half as complicated as the system of Ch'i circulation that later authors attributed to him. In this place it should be mentioned that the circulation of Ch'i or light is not practiced by all Taoist sects. Some adepts propose that the energy should be visualized to make it circulate, while others claim that it circulates quite happily on its own account, and that any visualization is useless interference. In their opinion an empty mind naturally restores the proper flow of energy, and distills the golden elixir of immortality. Lü Tung Pin, who attained liberation after the human spirit within him dissolved (this did not stop him from traveling and drinking) leads us to the next technical method to attain Tao: the art of refining breath.

Tuning the breath

In Taoist meditation and magick, the flow of the breath is one of the essential tools to calm and empty the mind. This concept can be found in many cultures. Best known is probably the highly complicated art of Pranayama Yoga. Similar methods were cultivated by certain Taoists who sought to refine their Ch'i energy for a number of purposes, such as martial arts practise or the attainment of health and immortality. Meditative breathing, however, is a long way from the attitudes taught by Yogis who aim at control of their respirative system. Indeed the very idea of control does not fit the meditative approach. To control something is to force it. The Taoists preferred to allow breath to return to its ultimate simplicity.

What is the primal breath? What is the natural way of breathing? How did you breathe before you were born? Far from seeking to obtain miraculous powers by manipulating breath, the early Taoist sages sought to return to the natural breathing of infants. To soothe and calm the mind, Lü Tung Pin advised that one should sit quietly and relaxed. Specific postures, like the Asanas of Yoga, are not required. In fact, these meditations can just as easily be practised while you stand, walk, dance or move in a Wu Shu form, provided it is done slowly and gently. It might be worth considering that the term *Sitting Still* is often used as a symbol for an attitude of Wu Wei, Not-Doing. You don't achieve an attitude of Not-Doing by forcing your body into an unmoving, cramped posture. More healthy is a posture that is so relaxed and at ease that body naturally does not wish to move about much. If it does, this is quite alright, and you should allow it.

The same goes for jolts of the muscles, swaying, shudders, shifts of weight and the like. The important issue is that body feels comfortable enough to be happy on its own and leaves your attention free to pursue other matters. Nothing is worse than an overly rigid attitude, be it in mind or body. When you sleep, your body also needs a bit of motion from time to time, as otherwise the muscles get badly cramped and the blood circulation suffers. This happens many times each night and you may never notice the motions as your attention is elsewhere. So, if you are wise you should allow your body to care for itself and focus your awareness on other matters.

In the beginning of meditation, so Lü Tung Pin advised, you could count breaths. This method is well known from several cultures. You can observe it in some older systems, as in Japanese martial arts, as well as in modern meditation, such as the Silva Method of Mind Control, or in hypnotherapy. Often enough, hypnotists tell their clients that they are going to count from ten to one backwards, and that with each number the client will relax, breath will flow easy and soft and the trance will become pleasant and deep. If this announcement is made in a congruent style, and if the hypnotist counts slowly, in a calm and soothing voice, such suggestions can lead to amazing results.

They give specific instructions to the deep mind and also provide a time-frame during which the desired change can happen. Its much easier to transform consciousness over a specific period than to expect a full change from one second to the other.

The main purpose of counting breaths is to give the mind something monotonous to do. I recommend that you use the counting method backwards, as this sort of counting, leading into a pleasant trance state, is not often needed in active daily life. Counting forward is often required, and it wouldn't really make you happy if it made you slip into a deep, calm trance state each time you had to count something. For instance you might count each breath that leaves your nostrils going from nine to zero, and then start again, and continue with this until a good trance develops. Or you could count backwards, say from 81, until you reach zero and a deep and calm trance state. If you imagine that you sink deeper with each breath, this may amplify the process. Use a calm inner voice, the sort of voice you would like to hear as your trance develops, and slow down. This is a highly literal description. People do *slow down* as they go into this sort of trance, and they also *speed up* as they leave trance and return to daily life consciousness. These terms are not just metaphors, they really describe what's going on.

For some mysterious reason, people tend to associate this sort of trance with the direction 'down', and though this is not really very meaningful or logical, it does happen to work. The actual technique you use to induce the trance is not important. What matters is that your attention is focused on something simple, dull and repetitive. It should be barely interesting enough to keep you from falling asleep. Find out what works for you and vary it from time to time, otherwise it will get too dull. If it becomes boring you should alter your approach a bit, otherwise your deep mind may get annoyed. Try to repeat a mantra or rehearse the alphabet. With a bit of practise you will find that reaching a comfortable trance gets easier each time you do it. Then, so Lü recommends, forget the counting and allow your breath to become more subtle. As the trance develops, breathing will change. I won't comment on how it changes, but you can be certain that breathing in trance differs from the way you breathe in waking awareness.

Lü Tung Pin wrote that you should reach the point where *breath and mind rest in each other and the thoughts are forgotten within the thinking*. This is a tricky idea - let me recommend that you don't make *any* effort. Maybe it happens naturally in its own good time. You don't have to be aware that it happens. Gradually, breath becomes soft and gentle, and eventually you won't notice it at all. This does not mean that you suffocate - not unless you really want to - but has to do with your attention. You can use your awareness of breath to calm the thoughts and emotions. Characteristically, this is done by not-doing. If you make an effort this won't get you anywhere. It is much more beneficial just to observe your breath as it flows. Allow your attention to dwell on the breathing. First, you'll be amazed how unsteady and irregular your breath is. This is typical for ordinary waking conscious-ness and for a couple of in-between states. It will be unsteady, but unsteady in a way that corresponds to your state of mind. If you are patient, your breath will calm down naturally. This is not achieved nor is it done - doing implies effort, and effort is an obstacle. Just be patient, or as Lü Tung Pin put it: '*Calm the primal awareness and the breath and trust in nature.*'

If you hurry at this stage you won't get anywhere. Instead, you may surprise yourself when you realize that you have always known that breathing is joy - and then forget the breathing as you return to the *Living Midnight*, to the Spirit of the Valley, to the sentience that was before you came to be. These magnificent metaphors hint at a state that lies beyond whatever you may attain, as there is no you to attain them. You may notice that the meditation recommended by Lü Tung Pin is a lot more detailed than the suggestions you can find in the writings of the earlier Taoists. Where these pioneers gave a few unrelated hints, Lü treats the way into trance as a process requiring several stages. For practical use, these can be summed up as follows. In stage one the body is rested comfortably, in stage two the mind is calmed using counting, in stage three breath and awareness are refined and become subtle and in stage four the practitioner returns to the primal simplicity and voidness, to the Living Midnight. In this stage body and self become vague and undefined, and though *You* are gone, there is something/nothing/whatever that remains perfectly conscious. Call it the True Self, the Tao, the Hun Tun, or better yet, don't call it anything. Such a description of stages in meditation may seem a bit overcomplicated, but it actually makes things easier for you. This is the importance of good syntax. When you know in what order to do something, it'll be a lot easier than doing it all at once.

Voiding the mind is easier if the mind and body are first calmed and relaxed. You may notice that the method of keeping attention on the breath until it becomes soft and subtle tends to combine itself with the method of focusing awareness on body and its sacred sites. To observe breathing is to observe where and how you breathe. Many Taoist arts, such as painting and Wu Shu, rely on belly breathing. This does not mean that your belly actually breathes - even Taoists have their lungs where other people keep theirs - but if you compress your lungs you can do this in several ways. Belly breathing means that your belly, the lower cinnabar field, moves as you breathe. Ideally, your belly moves inwards as you exhale and outwards as you draw fresh air and Ch'i energy into yourself. This is something of a problem for most people of our age. However, it can be learned, or rather remembered, as once there was a time, when you were an infant your breath used to move your belly naturally. The easiest way to remember belly breathing that I know of makes use of a small weight. Simply lie down on your back. Put a small weight on your belly and allow your arms to rest at your sides. The weight will help you feel the motion of your belly. Exhale gently. Can you feel the weight moving down? Now let your lungs draw in a good fresh breath. Again, is the weight moving up? Many people find this a bit unusual at first. Be patient. Sooner or later you'll get used to it, and your deep mind will make it a habit. This can be useful. Once you can do it when resting on your back you may enjoy to develop the skill of belly breathing while standing, walking and sitting. The last is hardest, as it requires a moderately upright position.

You can think of this as a form of meditation in itself. It also comes in handy if you wish to learn a martial art, to play a wind instrument or to dance and sing.

As there are lots of ways in which you can re-master belly breathing I won't go into details here. Suffice it to say that both the awareness of a hollow (or sacred center) and the refinement of breath are means to an end. You can allow them to help you along your way but as you follow your way you will come to a point where you won't need them any more. If there is any you, that is. The aim of technique is to transcend technique and to return to natural simplicity. Should you realize that you have forgotten breath or inner space give it a smile and proceed. It's a chance to go elsewhere and experience something new. The Living Midnight arises when you forget the world and yourself, when consciousness returns to the peaceful pleasure of the formless and unmanifest.

Some readers will notice that the basic form of Taoist meditation is similar to that used by certain Buddhist groups. Viewed from the outside, a meditating Taoist and a meditating Buddhist look pretty much alike. There are a couple of tiny differences that may be worth considering. For one thing, a good many Buddhists make use of breath awareness to keep their awareness steady in the present moment, in the Here and Now (whatever that may be). As Chögyam Trungpa Rinpoche kept emphasizing, each breath is unique. Each breath is now. By being aware of breath, you can sense the present time as intensely as possible. This leads to an awareness of all that is now, and provides a frame of mind that excludes a lot of other sensations, such as memories, daydreams, thinking of the future and the like. Both Buddhism and Taoism consider this sort of thinking as a disturbance of attention, as mind wandering and an obstacle.

This emphasis on the Now, however, is not usually found in classic Taoism. It can be made, and produces an interesting consciousness, but more often the breath is a means of refining and soothing awareness. Where so many Buddhists attempt to seize this moment of Now and to be fully aware of it, a lot of Taoists believe that the Tao appears when breath, intent, identity are forgotten. They do not especially care for the Now, nor for the Here, nor for the Whoever happens to perceive them. To insist on limiting awareness on any time or place (including the idea of the present) as such can be a charming way of getting trapped by one's own expectations. Perhaps this gives the impression that the Taoists could just as well have knocked themselves out with a bottle of scotch. Well, some of them do, and for their very own reasons, but so do some of the Buddhists. The difference in meditation technique, however, does not imply that the different techniques lead to different experiences. Beyond a certain point, all techniques become inconvenient and all goals, such as presence and absence, reveal their essential meaningless absurdity. Like the Buddhists, the Taoists rarely believe in the reality of the world (or themselves). This appears especially in the writings of Chuang Tsu and Lieh Tsu, both of whom were fond of dreaming, but not at all sure who did the dreaming, and what was the dream. The point is that if you insist on any consciousness, (such as the 'here and now'), you are likely to obsess yourself. On the other hand, the same happens when you try to force yourself to become void or absent-minded. The dream of the present is just as deluding as the dream of the absent. To set up an ideal is to limit yourself to a concept. To meditate for a purpose is to become tied to that purpose. As I am neither a Buddhist nor a Taoist (and wouldn't dream of limiting myself by sticking a label to my doing, unless it were a really funny one) you wont find me recommending one attitude or the other.

At times a meditation on the 'here and now' may be useful, at others a cultivation of oblivion. What good is it to insist? The essential issue is just what *you* require to deal with the phantasm of yourself. What will you think when you realize that there are options? How would you like more choices? What is there that the sages of antiquity overlooked or misunderstood? Meditation in itself is a convenience. This is a lie, but it may produce some fresh insights. Meditation is no better nor worse than any other activity. It is not especially beneficial, sacred or worthwhile *unless* you (complete this sentence in a way that gets you beyond whatever you used to believe before you came to laugh about it). If you believe that enlightenment, liberation or whatever are worth pursuing, go one step further and ask yourself what function these states are supposed to have. What is the function that meditation has for you? What is the use of this funny behaviour? Do you think that you'll be any happier once you happen to meditate successfully? No, I won't ruin your day by asking how you'll recognize that you are getting what you are searching for. There is not one road to enlightenment, there are as many as you chose to develop. But why insist on enlightenment at all? Why bother to strive? Enlightenment is just a word. So is liberation. As long as you believe that there is a goal, you'll be bound to it, and to your limited representation of it. How about several goals? How about goals that transcend your limited capacity of thinking of them at all? How about lots and lots of enlightening and liberating experiences, most of them unsuspected and therefore twice as surprising as you'll ever guess? Meditation may get you there, but it could also go further. When will you recognize that you have exceeded what you set out for, and find new horizons expanding everywhere? If you cultivate such beliefs, you may find that meditation, though but a convenience, can lead you to undefinable realms of perception that neither the Buddha nor Lao Tsu ever conceived or dared to dream of. The Tao that can be attained is not the eternal Tao. Can you hear the wind in the pines and the call of the white crane? It's as simple as that.

3 Immortals

An essay on the extension of consciousness.

Popular opinion, for what it's worth, tends to associate the practise of Taoism with the quest for an extended lifetime, or better still, for immortality itself. While there may be a little truth to this notion, there are so many misconceptions involved that we might as well tackle this knotty topic in all the detail it merits before we proceed to the practical fun section and the question of what good the immortals may be to you. Let us just set our time machine to the centuries, or even millennia, before the common era and find out what happens as we go along.

Our earliest references to immortal beings come from the works of Chuang Tsu and Lieh Tsu. They did not invent the idea of immortals, however, and merely retold legends that had been around for centuries. In one of the oldest, we go back to the very dawn of Chinese history, when the Yellow Emperor ruled the middle kingdom. According to a legend, this was from 2697 to 2597 BCE, but you don't have to believe in these dates unless you want to. The famous Yellow Emperor Huang Ti sought to extend his lifetime in order to make the most out of it. As a classical culture hero his main interest was to refine and improve the people who were under his sovereignty. For this purpose, he wrote a great tome on the art of medicine, which made much of the art of using plants and chemical substances. It also included advice on such topics as the cultivation of Ch'i, sexual hygiene and physical exercise. Whether or not the Yellow Emperor actually compiled or wrote this famous work remains an open question. Suffice it to say that he soon gained a reputation for being all-knowing, which flattered his ego mightily. As a busybody he worked hard at improving himself and his subjects. Year after year one reform followed another, and though this did not make people much happier, one could at least see that the Yellow Emperor was trying really hard. After 19 years of progressive politics Huang Ti heard that the famous sage Kuang Cheng Tse dwelled on a sacred mountain. What a great opportunity! Hurriedly, the Yellow Emperor travelled to the mountain, making as much haste as is possible for a regent and his court. With great eagerness, the Yellow Emperor approached the aged saint, and he said:

I have heard, O master, that you have the perfect Tao. May I dare to enquire what the Tao consists of? I intend to make use of the influence of heaven and earth so that the five grains thrive and the people find nourishment. I desire to control the forces of yin and yang to protect the living beings. How may I do so?' Kuang Cheng Tse laughed when he heard this. Shaking his head he replied: '*What you intend to use is the primal unity of all things. What you desire to control are the forces that divide. And what do you do? As long as you have ruled, the clouds have released their rain before they were full enough. Leaves fell before they were ready, sun and moon have lost their glow. Your goals are those of a clever speaking opportunist. How can you ever understand the perfect Tao?*

Deeply shaken, the Yellow Emperor departed. He sent his entourage to the court. He gave up his title and his authority. Totally on his own, he disappeared into the splendour of the mountains. In the desolation of misty crags and pinnacles, close to an icy waterfall, the former Yellow Emperor built a shaky hut and slept on a bed of grasses. For three months he dwelled in loneliness. Then he returned to the sacred mountain and sought out Kuang Cheng Tse once more. The aged sage thought that the Yellow Emperor looked much improved in his weatherworn state.

'*Come*' said the old adept, '*I will tell you of the Tao. The nature of the perfect Tao is hidden in the deep, its height disappears in darkness. Step where nothing can be seen, where nothing can be heard, rest your soul in stillness and the physical self will acquire its own shape. Be quiet, be pure, do not exhaust the body, do not tangle your life energy. You will endure. When the eye does not see and the ear does not hear and the heart does not know, the soul will preserve body and the physical self endures. Preserve what is within and leave out what is outside, the craving for knowledge misleads. Then I will place you on the pinnacle of great light, I will lead you to the source of yang, and also I will guide you through the gate of the deep darkness where you will find the source of yin...guard and preserve your self and everything will thrive of itself.*'

So the Yellow Emperor learned from the old sage and disappeared into the mountains to refine the Tao. He soon forgot about reforms and good intentions. He forgot all that he had assumed to know previously. He became simple and happy. When he had forgotten himself, the Tao appeared. The former Yellow Emperor broke out laughing. How could he have striven for so long? What appeared as the Tao had always been there. Then he fell asleep and he dreamed that he flew to the fabled land Hua Su. This country has no ruler, and its people have no desire. All goes on its own accord, everything develops naturally. The people of this country do not cling to life nor do they fear death. Beauty and ugliness do not cloud their minds, valleys and mountains do not slow their step. They cultivate no likes or dislikes, they walk on air, they rest in empty space, they move in the force of the spirit. Then the Yellow Emperor woke. He had found the ultimate Tao when he had ceased from searching for it, but as it so happens could not express it. So he returned to his throne and his function in the world. For another twenty-eight years the Yellow Emperor sat on the dragon throne between heaven and earth. He cultivated the Tao and did nothing. Consequently, there was nothing that was not cultivated. The state improved, the people thrived and the middle kingdom became almost as perfect as the country Hua Su.

This account, compiled mainly from anecdotes given by Lieh Tsu and Chuang Tsu around the third century BCE contains several basic ideas connected with the dream of immortality. For one thing, it introduces the figure of the sage who dwells in splendid isolation in the remote mountain ranges. The very word for immortal, *hsien*, is composed out of the characters mountain and human, making the immortal simply a mountain dweller. Kuang Cheng Tse, while still around as a human being, comes also close to the way in which a lot of immortals are said to appear. Such beings could look like shabby outcasts, living on a handful of rice, wearing tattered robes and celebrating a remarkable lack of manners. Often, such people were thought to be able to use superhuman forces and to work miracles. Chuang Tsu, fooling a lot of literal minded folk, describes such recluses in a famous passage:

' ...*on the mountain Ku She lives a man who appears like a spirit. His flesh is like ice and snow, his attitude like that of a virgin. He does not eat the fruits of the earth but gains nourishment from air and dew. He rides over the clouds on a chariot drawn by dragons, he travels beyond the four seas. This being is totally idle. Nevertheless it makes the harvest grow and prevents that the things decay...*'

Other authors elaborated on this theme. While it is doubtful if they actually bothered to spend a few days in the mountains to gain some first hand experience of mountain dwellers and the conditions they live in, they certainly extended the myth and improved the hermit's reputation. What would you make of a tale that informs you that immortals can fly to the highest palaces of the ninth heaven on the back of a dragon or a crane, have breakfast with the Queen Mother of the West, dance with the dragon king's daughter in the depth of the ocean, and return from their journey before their tea has cooled? We can approach such miraculous tales in several ways.

The easiest interpretation is to take them literally. Yes, there are immortal beings around who have perfected themselves to an extent that makes physical immortality a matter of course. This attitude has been taken by a lot of simple souls, the very sort of persons who believe that immortality might be a nice thing well worth having. From this point of view, the body and the personality can endure forever, the gods and ghosts are tangible and real and there is no difference between the planes of existence.

Another interpretation is cultivated by intellectuals who do not strictly believe in the immortality of anything. Yes, there are immortals around, but this is just a metaphor for a spiritual truth and should not be taken literally. To say that they fly through space on enchanted beasts is to symbolize their freedom from limitation, for example, and to visit a deity is to realize one's own relation to abstract divine forces that exist within oneself. The flowery language of the old sages is suggestive in a splendid poetic style, but would not require anyone to take its allegories seriously.

Yet another interpretation comes from those who have studied magick and shamanism. This one says that while the tale may be a metaphor, so is the reality. Lots of sorcerers worldwide have flown to the height of heaven, the depths of the ocean, or to the dwelling places of deities and demons. Generally, such journeys take place in the imagination. While all of these visions may be metaphors they are also quite real to the traveler, who returns from such journeys with wider understanding and deeper wisdom and transforms the world in the process. Who says that the dream world, the astral plane or the world of magickal imagination are more or less real than the material world where you have a crazed old hermit squatting in a cave? Thus, a dragon can be a metaphor but it is also a reality. A deity can be a metaphor but also a living entity or the personification of an abstract force. And what is the sage's personality but a convenient metaphor that allows Tao to manifest in a human form?

While it is not the purpose of these lines to decide for one or another of these interpretations, you would do well to recall that each of them has its adherents, whose influence combined to produce the complicated myth of the immortals. That this myth has many levels of meaning to many people does not make it easier to digest, but you may find that without this multiplicity of meaning it wouldn't work half as elegantly. There are several different types of immortals woven into the complicated texture of Chinese myth, depending on the attitude cultivated by the storyteller.

Let's take another look at the so-called first emperor, Chin Shih Huang Ti, who made a name for himself by uniting six kingdoms by conquest (and forcing a number of others into submission) in the second half of the third century BCE. This took him about 25 years of almost continuous warfare, a process ending in the first appearance of a united China and in the bizarre gesture that the first emperor assumed the name of the legendary Yellow Emperor (Huang Ti), whom you have already encountered, and who was so venerated that until the reign of Chin Shih Huang Ti nobody had dared to use this name. Chin Shih Huang Ti dared, and went quite beyond it. Today he is famous for a number of amazing reforms (he standardized language, weights, currency and even the axles of chariots) for megalomaniac architecture (the great wall was largely built at his command, and so was an extensive system of canals) and for his ruthless political reforms, which involved a transformation of the older feudal system, the mass execution of Confucian scholars and one of the most drastic book burning campaigns in human history.

As he grew older, the emperor steadily became more paranoid. This had lots of good reasons, as he was well aware that he was one of the most unpopular regents in Chinese history. In order to evade attempts at assassination he had his 270 palaces linked by covered passages. This made it rather hard for his foes to observe the motions of the emperor, who moved from palace to palace like a ghost in the night and rarely slept in the same place twice. Somehow the notion of being invisible had a great appeal for Chin Shih Huang Ti, as it made him seem more than human. In the depths of his heart the first emperor was a man torn by conflicting beliefs. Like most people of his time he believed in an afterlife. This required preparation in the form of an elaborate tomb, and indeed, as soon as he mounted the throne (at the age of 13), an army of workers began to toil at the grave monument. The grave took 36 years to build, and required a work-force of 700,000 conscripts. Today it is one of the most famous tombs in the world. No doubt you have seen pictures of it, and of the thousands of larger than life terracotta soldiers and horses it included. Now the terracotta soldiers were just an extra to the monument. The emperor himself came to rest in an earth mound fifteen stories high. His corpse in a copper coffin was placed on an ornate dragon-ship that floated on a river of mercury in a miniature landscape that represented the whole of China. There were two rivers of mercury in the tomb, representing the Yellow River and the Yangtse, and an ingenious mechanical system made these rivers flow into an artificial ocean. So tells us the historian Ssu-Ma Ch'ien, who wrote a century after the death of the first emperor.

Such burial customs show a distinctly magical thinking. In a sense Chin Shih Huang Ti had his corpse placed within the centre of a sacred model of the world he used to rule. He took models of thousands of his warriors along, and a number of craftsmen, who were buried alive in the tomb. There is an ancient Chinese belief that ancestors ought to be buried in places that enjoy a suitable flow of Ch'i energy, so that the ancestor may benefit from the energy. Such an ancestor makes a powerful spirit who is likely to support and aid the family. To understand the full importance of this custom you might consider that the worship of ancestors was probably the strongest religion of Neolithic China. In a similar sense, Chin Shih Huang Ti had himself buried in a self-designed magical model of all China. What place of power could surpass the totality of the land? The dragon boat identifies him with the force of heaven itself and the mercury is one of the most valued substances of Taoist alchemy, as it was supposed to extend life if prepared properly.

All of this makes it likely that the first emperor wanted to continue his luxurious life in some sort of otherworld and to become an ancestor with more power than any other. On the other hand he did not want to die at all, and was crazy with the hope of attaining immortality. In his case this did not mean solitary meditation in the wild mountains, nor was he the sort of person who would practise austerities or listen to a crazed hermit praising the beauty of the rose coloured clouds of dawn. His idea was to become immortal using more direct means. For this purpose he employed countless adepts and sorcerers who were to produce the golden pill, the red cinnabar medicine and similar substances that were thought to heal all ills and extend life forever. All elixirs and potions were carefully tested, and a good many alchemists executed when their products did not meet the emperor's expectations. In this matter he was a cunning and suspicious man, unlike a lot of aristocrats and even a couple of later emperors who attempted to extend their lifetime and accidentally poisoned themselves in the process.

In Chin Shih Huang Ti's case the medicines did not avail anything. Next, the first emperor, who had done some reading, decided that he needed to get the real recipe from a real immortal. From the works of Lieh Tsu (most of which he certainly neither understood nor valued) he derived the idea that there are several mysterious paradises to the north or east of China, where people dwell who have realized the Tao and become immortal. Enthusiastically, the first emperor sent out a fleet of ships to search for these sacred spaces. After a lengthy quest, the officer in charge, a captain Hsu, returned to the court with excellent news. He had, so he said, met an immortal sage on a distant island. He had offered costly gifts to the immortal, and told him of the emperor's desire for the elixir of immortality. Sadly, the immortal had taken offence. 'Are these trifles all that your lord can afford?' thundered the sage. 'Let me apologize sincerely' said the enterprising captain Hsu, 'what is your desire?' 'Strong young men, young maidens and craftsmen of all trades' was the answer of the immortal.

Chin Shih Huang Ti was beside himself with delight. He ordered captain Hsu to set out for another journey. In his company were some 3000 of the best women, men and artisans that could be found. On an auspicious day they left China for the island of the immortal, and were never seen again. Possibly they all travelled to paradise, but more likely they came to settle in Japan. There is a monument in Japan that bears the name of a Taoist who was on board and who died in 179 BCE. Who knows if the crafty captain Hsu did not invent the charming immortal on his mysterious island, rather than return home with a tale of failure and the prospect to die for it very slowly. The highly disappointed Chin Shih Huang Ti had to make do with his paranoid secrecy and his bombastic tomb. This wasn't as good as immortality but it was better than nothing. When he finally died his ministers managed to keep their regent's death secret for so long that the corpse that came to rest in the mound was more than ripe for the deep. In fact, they had to transport it between wagons full of rotten fish in order to cover the emperor's own aroma. Within a few years the first emperor's dynasty was violently extinguished and the historians soon turned Chin Shih Huang Ti into the most unpopular regent who ever sat on the dragon throne.

The first emperor was not the only person who believed in the possibility of obtaining immortality in the flesh. Over the centuries an amazing amount of people came to believe in this fabulous prospect. I suspect that this was a revival of a piece of folk religion that came to be included in Taoist beliefs. If you study the works attributed to Lao Tsu, Lieh Tsu and Chuang Tsu you will find several texts that frown on the idea of physical immortality. When these authors spoke of immortals, they generally spoke of beings who ought to be classed as spirits rather than humans. While folk belief turned Lao Tsu into an immortal, and then into a deity, Chuang Tsu made a point of refering to the old sage's death, and to the fact that it was an inevitable and natural event. To be born and to die is part of the flow of the Tao. Even practices that aimed at improving health and extending one's lifespan seemed highly suspicious to those authors. If they involved making an effort they were possibly not in tune with the changeful flow of Tao, and better avoided. Of course this did not imply that becoming old was a mistake.

The error lay in striving for old age, regardless of the means. When

Taoists came to live for unusually long periods this was attributed to the fact that they had become so simple and natural that their health had recovered from all abuse, and they had returned to their natural length of life in the process. It might be useful to recall that in ancient Chinese belief, the duration of life was preordained by heaven. While the number of years one was entitled to was fixed, there did exist the possibility to influence it. People who were on good terms with the heavenly or hellish bureaucracy could get their numbers improved occasionally, and likewise, persons who abused the decrees of heaven by committing sins could expect that their life-expectation was drastically reduced. For many of the early Taoists the idea of growing overly old, or worse yet, of becoming physically immortal, held very little attraction. Those sages did not believe in the reality of the world nor in the reality of their own personality, so why should they bother to remain incarnate and tied to the illusion? The immortality of the personal identity is surely one of the most terrifying prospects that people ever invented. Consequently, some of the most desperate seekers for immortality were hardly concerned with Taoist refinement but simply power-hungry aristocrats attempting to extend the length of their delusions. Quite a few of them studied the works of the ancient sages and took them literally. Consider the following.

A number of Taoist manuals taught the secrets of mystical refinement in a highly obscure language. In such works you can find instructions on the art of producing the golden pill of immortality in the alchemical oven, a complicated procedure involving the distillation of mercury, lead, cinnabar, mysterious mushrooms, jade, nephrite, costly metals, dragon pearls and even more obscure substances. Such ingredients had to be refined and distilled in a number of complicated ovens, furnaces and cauldrons over lengthy periods. This may remind you of the joys of European alchemy, which is quite as obscure and misleading if taken literally. Several classics of Chinese alchemy were translated into Arabic and subsequently into European languages, usually by people who did not understand what they were talking about, and confused the science of chemistry with alchemical meditation.

The alchemy of the Taoists required, first of all, that one knew the secret meaning of its vocabulary. This was easier said than done. Mercury, for example, could be a term meaning the male sexual fluids, while cinnabar could refer to their female counterparts. The golden elixir pill can be a metaphor for the natural true self. The medicine of immortality a term for Ch'i energy. Sometimes the cauldron is a part of the body or body as a whole and the firing process a code name for the art of refining breath until it becomes the 'true', 'primal' and 'original' breath, free of control or conscious interference, and the gateway to the Tao.

When the elixir was refined nine times this could be a reference to nine stages of meditative practice. This is just one interpretation of these metaphors and there are plenty of others. Sadly, the very writers who hid their secrets in such flowery language never bothered to standardize their terminology, and so there are plenty of secret texts that attribute other meanings to the ingredients of the life-conferring broth. Those poor fools who actually ingested mercury, cinnabar and lead soon destroyed their health in the very attempt to improve it.

Or take the Taoist expression that one should create a spiritual embryo within the ovens. Magically speaking, such an embryo can mean a new personality, i.e. a new state of consciousness. Some people took this to mean that the medicine of long life should contain a human foetus, and went to extremes to gain and cook one. Others tried to live on pine sap as the pine symbolizes a long life. Other popular medicines included powdered jade, stalactites, turtle-shells and arsenic. Such tragic delusions hardly concern us here. They are merely indications of the obsessive striving of certain folk to avoid the approach of death and the dissolution of their sorry little ego.

More interesting is a school of thought that sought for immortality by the ingestion of sexual fluids. This idea may well have been influenced by some of the more secretive systems of left hand Tantra, which made an art out of the cultivation of certain sexual fluids and energies. One of the foundations of Taoist inner alchemy are the three essentials. You can find plenty of references to them in the writings of Taoist sages, starting in the early centuries of the common era and finding a definition in the writings of that famous immortal, Lü Tung Pin. The three essences, or treasures, are broadly speaking:

Ching. This term can be translated using such words as essence, vitality, or the constructive, manifesting force. Ching in its crudest form appears in the sexual fluids, on a more subtle level it is the force that materializes body, while on a cosmic level Ching is the tendency of the original void to transform into the ten thousand things.

Ch'i. This is the life force itself, the energy of change, the motion of the heavenly bodies and more. On the microcosmic level, Ch'i refers to bioenergy. This force is generated by all living beings, it is also produced by the interaction of heaven and earth, and generally results in activity. To understand this concept you could imagine that all living beings, while generating Ch'i, also move through an immense and all-inclusive field of this energy. You wouldn't find the same quality of Ch'i in all places, times and beings, but you will always encounter Ch'i, as without it, death occurs instantly. On a larger scale, Ch'i is the energy that keeps the universe going, so you shouldn't take it personally. It can be compared to the *Te*, the magical power cultivated by the sage.

Shen. This is a reference to what might be termed spirit, or life-imbuing original consciousness. It is not personal spirit, rather you might imagine Shen as an unpersonal, all pervading sentience. In its crudest form, Shen can refer to mind and reason, or to the concept of your self. More subtly, Shen is the self that is when all personality ceases to be, the formless, nameless awareness that is truly immortal as it was neither born nor can it die. On a cosmic scale, Shen is the great void of the beginning, and the force that dissolves phenomena and returns the ten thousand things to their origin.

Though these explanations are full of inaccurancies, they may suffice to give you a workable idea of the essences that Taoist alchemy sought to refine. To understand them more fully, I would like to recommend the excellent compilation *Vitality, Energy, Spirit. A Taoist Sourcebook* by T. Cleary. In this essay it may be enough to say that the alchemists sought a refinement of themselves by conserving and nourishing Ching, Ch'i and Shen. Further, they sought to refine the Ching into Ch'i and the Ch'i into Shen, equalling a return to primal voidness and simplicity. You could call this enlightenment (a Buddhist concept) or immortality, but essentially, either of them only occurs when there is no-one left who could become enlightened or immortal. Of course popular belief could not cope with such tricky concepts and produced a number of methods that were loosely based on a simplified model of the three treasures.

Take Ching for instance. A common belief had it that humans only have a limited amount of sexual fluids and if these were wasted, the result would be weak offspring, poor health and early death. This made a number of teachers praise the virtues of chastity to an extent that spells restriction (and isn't very much in accord with the Tao).

Such teachings gained popularity when they were taught to the emperors and nobles. Well, the emperors were in a position to have good reason to fear overmuch loss of semen. For one thing, too many royal children could cause plenty of political problems. For another, the *Li Chi*, or *Book of Rites*, ensured that every concubine under the age of fifty had the right to have intercourse every five days. Considering that even low nobility kept upwards of thirty wives and concubines, this certainly implies considerable strain on the husbands' semen production unless ejaculation was carefully avoided (see R. Tannahill's study *Sex in History*). The ability to make love ten times a night without loss of semen has much to do with a social code that demands such feats of virility. Various adepts composed detailed manuals that taught retention of semen to the aristocrats, and these teachings soon resulted in the mistaken impression that Taoist lovemaking depends on keeping and storing one's sexual fluids at all costs.

To avoid loss of semen became something of an obsession and some authors went so far to claim that each ejaculation would imply a reduction of one's life-expectation. It also produced the idea that women can improve their health and length of life by making their partner ejaculate.

There is a bizarre tale mentioned by Eberhard and Blofeld (who wasn't very happy about it) claiming that the divine Hsi Wang Mu (Xiwangmu), the Queen Mother of the West, was originally a human being. Under unspecified circumstances she collected the semen of a thousand healthy young men and became immortal. Nowadays you can meet her in a cave on the fabulous K'un Lun mountain where she appears as a beautiful lady with a splendid jade headdress or as a fiend with tangled hair, tiger teeth, a panther's tail and the disagreeable habit of eating people. She has become the custodian of the herb or mushroom that confers immortality but most of those who desire it are immediately devoured. Hsi Wang Mu may be one of the oldest surviving Chinese deities. Her cult can be traced to the centuries before the common era. Nowadays she has assumed the role of a mother goddess, mainly due to a reinterpretation of her name. The character Mu used to specify a mysterious otherworldly realm or a real country in the fabulous west of which she was queen. As early as the Han dynasty the meaning of Mu had been forgotten and so it was replaced by the similar sounding Mu (meaning mother) though this was spelt with a different character.

On the other hand there were a number of men who sought to extend their own lifetime by retaining semen and feeding on the sexual juices of their wives and concubines, a practice that might be related to the eating of the so called cinnabar elixir. Others saw sexuality as a useful means to strengthen health, such as Chang Chüeh, a Taoist of the late Han period, who founded a popular cult that praised promiscuity and indulged in group-sex orgies at new and full moon to produce deliverance from guilt for the devotees. This organization, called the Yellow Turbans after the scarves worn around the heads of its members, was soon and violently suppressed by the government.

Of course this simply drove the organization underground where it may still flourish to this day. There is nothing like suppression to increase the romantic flair of a philosophical or religious movement. To keep things in a proper perspective you should consider that unlike the Buddhists, many Taoists were married, and unlike the aristocrats, they generally did not keep dozens of wives and concubines. Early Taoism is in favour of lovemaking as first of all, it can be a road to heaven and second, all forms of restriction and repression tend to upset body and mind. To this day there are many Taoist adepts who see celibacy and retaining of semen as an artificial restriction interfering with the motion of Tao. Some even claim that Ching is wasted, no matter whether fluids are lost or not, whenever sexual lust becomes an obsessive need. In their opinion it does not matter whether semen is ejaculated or held back, as the fundamental principle in it, the Ching, is lost anyway (see Cleary 1996).

To make use of other people's Ching to increase one's own health is frowned upon by a good many Taoist writers. Others have different opinions and so far there is no consensus regarding the matter. Or take the common idea that Ch'i needs to be stored and guarded. Some authors treat Ch'i as if it were a limited resource, and advise their readers to conserve it by closing the orifices of the body. Others believe that Ch'i is present everywhere and the way to cultivate it is to open up to its universal flow. Both attitudes can easily be supported by quotations from the works of Lao Tsu, the first by reference to the passage that advises the saint-like ruler to close the gates and apertures, the other by those lucid lines that state: *The saint does not hoard. As he acts for others he has more for himself, as he gives to others he gains more for himself.* Chapter 31 (81).

Some advise that physical exercise, such as Ch'i Kung (Quigong) and certain forms of gentle Wu Shu generate and refine Ch'i, thereby producing health and longevity, while others propose that any deliberate exercise, being of an unspontaneous nature, interferes with Tao and reduces health. In these matters I wouldn't dream of voicing an opinion. Suffice it to say that people and their needs differ, and that one person's elixir of immortality may well be another's poison.

But let us return to the main path, the broad road of this essay. For millennia, people in China were convinced that people can become immortal and that such immortals can occasionally, if very rarely, be encountered on earth. This belief took several shapes. Some prefered to believe in a flesh and blood immortality while others saw immortality as something that happens as a side result when awareness is sufficently refined to transcend the personality. This sort of immortality could mean that the physical body was still subject to age, injury, disease and death, but that the spirit transcended all of them. It would be easy to take this as a dispute between factions believing in immortal flesh against immortal spirit, but such a division is misleading as it proposes an either/or decision. In a worldview that sees neither flesh nor spirit as separate, nor necessarily especially real, such a distinction hardly makes sense. Likewise, there seem to be several sorts of immortals around.

For one thing, the term immortal can be an honorific title that is kindly given to advanced Taoists or to those who are especially old. This does not mean that anyone takes it very seriously, least of all the person referred to. In a similar fashion good manners demanded that everyone at the court pretended that the present emperor lives for ten thousand years. It was simply not polite to consider that the son of heaven would eventually die. If this option had to be discussed it was carefully framed as 'after ten thousand years' which made it sound as if it would never happen anyway.

Another sort of immortal can be thought of as a purely spiritual being that only appears in the world of mortals from time to time to help, give advice or righten a wrong, usually by not doing. A good example can be found in the *Pingyaozhuan*, where you can find the Bare Feet Immortal incarnating on earth as the emperor Renzong. He did this at the command of heaven as conditions on earth had become unbearable and the dear immortal had been unwise enough to let it show that he felt compassion for humanity. This concept comes close to the Buddhistic idea of a Bodhisattva, i.e. an enlightened person who has chosen not to disappear into the non-manifest but to re-incarnate to help all living beings to attain liberation. This type of immortal generally appears to live an almost human life and upon death tends to leave a dead body behind. What is also implied is the idea of re-incarnation, a notion that is not particularly common to early Taoism but became more popular under the influence of Buddhism. There are legends that claim that the Yellow Emperor reincarnated as Lao Tsu, for instance, but this does not necessarily imply that he did it perforce (as the Hindu model of re-incarnation would have it) or that it happens to everyone. Indeed there are plenty of different re-incarnation theories around, ranging from unhappy bondage to voluntary choice.

Other immortals seem to appear like apparitions. They seem real enough to the people who meet them but then again they only seem to come to earth for short periods. When they need a body they assume its form, this is a great deal easier than being born, growing up and all the rest of it. Some of their good humour can be accounted for by the fact that they don't have to go to work for years and years, unless they really want to.

Other immortals are not human at all. Fox and monkey spirits, to name just two talented beasts, have a certain aptitude for becoming immortal, and the same is said of the toad with three legs, of deer, tigers and rams (see the *Journey to the West* by Wu Cheng En.) Of foxes it is said that they can easily transform into human shape of either sex in order to make love and gain the Ching of healthy people. Luo Guanzhong and Feng Menglong, both of them experts on the topic, inform us that foxes that desire to assume human shape need parts of a human skull. They place the bone on their own head and pray to the moon as sincerely as they can (which is usually not very). If the decree of heaven accords with the transformation, the fox becomes a human being (if only outwardly) of the same sex as the skull worn on the head. Bowing forty-nine times to the moon fixes the spell. Then a handful of leaves is turned into proper clothes and already our fox is ready to go into the world to work mischief. Not only is there a stunning charm to such foxy people, but they can easily pass themselves off as living Buddhas or Taoist saints and work miracles of questionable nature. When a fox has gained enough Ching (and from ten people nine and a half can't resist their sex appeal) this subtle essence can be refined into Ch'i, then into Shen, and already our cunning fox is well on the way to immortality. A fox who has lived for a thousand years, so it is said, has a chance of becoming a heavenly fox.

The last emperor of the Shang dynasty, a certain Chou Sin, was half-heartedly worshipping in a temple when a sudden gust of wind moved the curtains in front of the shrine of the primal serpent deity Nü Kua. Seeing the golden image of the goddess, he began to entertain lascivious fantasies about her instead of keeping his mind on the ceremony. Before he left he wrote a tasteless poem on the wall of the temple, to the effect that he wouldn't mind taking here home as a concubine. This offended the goddess so much that she decided to put a stop to the dynasty. Ordinarily, most deities don't mind the odd lustful thought but coming from a tyrant renowned for his cruelty things were somewhat different. Nu Kua sent a heavenly fox with nine tails to earth in the shape of a beautiful woman. The emperor soon fell under her spell and made her his consort. Pretending to be a human being the nine-tailed fox stimulated the emperor's cruelty to unsurpassed extremes. At her suggestion, the emperor impoverished the country in order to build a luxurious terrace. He had a lake of wine, a garden of flesh (or rather dead meat), a thriving snake-pit and a number of ingenious new torture instruments. The ministers, the nobles and the philosophers complained about this dismal state. One after the other they were cruelly tortured to death until finally the exiled 'King Wu' attacked the realm and brought an end to the imperial reign of terror. King Wu or 'King War', was the title of Ji Fa, the Duke of Chou, whom you met earlier as one of the most prominent authors of the *I Ching*. In spite of his title he seems to have been a humble and peaceful character who was more or less installed on the throne by the crafty magician Jiang Ziya. With the help of the nine-tailed fox Nü Kua brought the Shang dynasty to an end. In typical Taoist fashion she accelerated the emperor's downfall, knowing full well that power, once it becomes excessive, reverts into weakness.

In Chinese myth, foxes are often ambiguous creatures. Not all of them are a threat to humans. Some foxes teach poetry and martial arts to their human lovers. Other stories of foxes make much of their power to lead hermits, students or sages into temptation. In these tales the prime motivation of the foxes is to gain a good store of high quality Ching. Could these cheerful tales be a reference to some obscure cult blending sexual vampirism with beast-form sorcery? Of course the myths frown on this sort of enterprise and comment that the immortality gained by such means is only of a temporary nature, barely lasting for a couple of aeons at a time, but who knows what a really clever fox may learn if given such a lot of time?

Our next topic is the sort of behaviour you can expect from immortals, should you happen to encounter them. A legend states that Liu Hai became a statesman at the age of fifty. He served the Chin dynasty with all his skill and led a life that was full of dutiful work and untiring effort. One fine day he was amazed to see two aged men walking into his palace without any concern for the guards. When he asked for their desire, the strange pair demanded a coin and ten eggs. This did not seem too great a request to Liu Hai, and he had the items brought. 'Watch this!' said the elders, and set the coin spinning on the ground, 'does this look risky?' 'Certainly not!' replied Liu Hai. Then to his amazement the two old guys proceeded to balance an egg on top of the spinning coin. They set the egg spinning and balanced another one on top. Egg after egg was added until a total of ten eggs were merrily spinning on top of the coin. 'What are you doing?' shouted Liu Hai, 'this isn't risky, it's madness!' 'You must be joking, your Honour,' was the reply, 'it's not half as risky as being a statesman.' Liu Hai felt his sanity slipping away. What had seemed so important to him a moment ago ceased to make sense any more. Throwing away his official hat he ran to join the two immortals and together they disappeared from the world of yellow earth.

Today he is not only known as an immortal but also as a helpful deity. You can easily recognize his picture, as he is usually shown as a young man whirling a string of coins and playing with the famous toad of three legs. This toad is another immortal. She used to be the woman Ch'ang-O who stole the elixir of immortality from her husband and subsequently became a moon goddess. To this day toads are connected with the moon in Chinese symbolism, but also with wealth and occasionally with the joys of the bridal bed.

The idea that humans can become quasi-divine immortals may be acceptable to modern minds but the thought that they can also become deities is not that easy to stomach. Nevertheless it is a common notion in Chinese religion, and one that cannot be explained away as euhemerization. Where several medieval European writers did their best to explain old and unwanted pagan deities as human beings with amazing sorcerous reputations, Chinese faith finds it only natural that unusual humans may become divine eventually. This can happen while incarnate - there is a lot of possession by spirits and deities in folk religion - but more commonly it happens after death. The highest deity of heaven, the famous Jade Emperor, used to be a human being, and the same goes for a lot of other divinities including the very god of death and all his officials. I have no idea if this concept is an old tradition or a recent religious innovation, but whatever it may be, it has been a common thought for several centuries. The idea behind this faith may well be that a god or spirit who used to be human cares for the needs and problems of those human beings who invoke her or him. Indeed, the more recently a deity was incarnate in human form the more compassionate and understanding it is thought to be. This produces a curious attitude in the worshippers.

The old and majestic deities of prehistory are also the least concerned when it comes to human affairs. Most of them have been in office for so long that they have very little personality, and consequently few tales can be told about them. Much closer to the heart of the people are deities and immortals who have transcended humanity only a couple of centuries ago, or who tend to appear as humans from time to time. This keeps them in touch with the world of phenomena and makes them more or less reliable allies of their worshippers. Yuan Mei's splendid compilation *What Confucius Did Not Mention* (c. 1792), even proposes that all deities were originally dead humans, but then this work proposes just about anything in order to annoy Confucian scholars.

In Chinese religion the gap between gods and humans is much smaller than in a lot of religions, provided one can detect a gap at all. In this model the difference between life-forms, spirits and deities is not one of nature but of degree. It may be worthwhile to contemplate what changes are possible in a reality where every entity is totally free to transform into other classes of being. What advantages arise out of this belief? And how can you blend them into your magick?

The Eight Immortals

Of all the hundreds of immortals that haunt the lofty mountains and tangled forests of Chinese mythology perhaps the best known are the famous Eight Immortals. This group of happy sages is one of the most popular topics in Chinese art. You can find them, either on their own or in the full group of eight on priceless works of art, in temples, shrines, restaurants and wherever people feel the need for special blessings. They are even present on some of the bills issued by the Bank of Hell. This is a form of money that is usually burned at Chinese funerals in order to ensure that the deceased has a good bank account on the other side. I find this idea a splendid custom. If you are worried about your old age pension, invest in the Bank of Hell, it is a lot more

reliable than financial investments in the human world. Also, the bills are very pretty and they usually have so many zeros on them that you hardly know what to call such numbers.

The Eight Immortals are a mixed group. They were not invented in one go but blended together over the centuries. This explains why there is some overlap regarding the functions and appearance. Not all of the eight are equally popular, but all of them are expressions of the many faces assumed in the manifestation of Tao, and this is why I shall introduce them to you now. Who knows, maybe you have met one or another of them before. As with the deities, all of the immortals used to be human before they transcended their personality and became pure spirit. Some of them were even historical figures, but they soon got over that when they attained Tao. There are plenty of tales told about them, not all of them in agreement with each other. I'll give a brief synopsis of their nature and deeds based on the inspiring writings of Wilhelm, Eberhard, Kwok Man Ho, Cleary, Blofeld and on direct contact with the immortals themselves.

Chung Li Ch'uan may well be one of the oldest of the group and is usually shown as a laughing man with a formidable naked belly holding a magical fan. This fan has the power that it can raise the winds and gales, it can make the ocean churn, the waves sweep and the tempest roar. This is one of the elder types of fan that looks a bit like a human lung. You might take it as a symbol of the power of breath. The fan has not only vitalizing power, referring to the Taoist skill of refining Ch'i using breathing exercises, but it can also bring the dead to life. Likewise, a large belly is not necessarily a sign of fat but represents the adepts power to store Ch'i energy in the lower cinnabar field.

One legend makes him an alchemist of the Han dynasty (either early Han, 207 BCE-9 CE or later Han, 23-220 CE) who transformed mercury and lead into noble metals and became immortal by ingesting a mixture of gold and cinnabar. Another tale portrays him as a general of the Sung dynasty (960-1278 CE) who fought the Liao people of

Chung Li Ch'uan

North China. These were supported by Lü Tung Pin who later became Chung's pupil and friend. Confusing as it may seem, a common tradition makes Chung Li Ch'uan a general of the Han dynasty who fought against the Tibetans and suffered unexpected defeat. Escaping from the battlefield he chose to become a hermit. He is said to have stated that it is easier to kill a thousand enemies than to master one's own passions.

Yet another tale makes him a former judge, who happened to meet the famous Lü Tung Pin during a trial. In the circle of later heaven, his sign is Thunder, The Arousing, in the east. His name consists of the following elements: Chung is the family name. It can mean *a measure (a cup)*, as well as *to treasure, to love* and *to unite*. Li is *to divide*, the character refers to the brilliantly yellow *oriole*, to *radiance* and *light* and to the trigram *Li*. Chuan can mean *weight, to measure* and *power*, as well as *using the circumstances*, possibly *opportunism*.

Han Hsiang Tsu is a flute player. Starting as a historical person, he used to be the nephew of the famous scholar Han Yu who lived in the early ninth century. He was so attracted by the solitary ways of the mountain dwellers that he gave up life in human society and retired into the wilderness while he was still a young man. In pictures he is generally shown in youthful appearance, playing a transverse or more rarely a vertical flute. Often he used to seek out lonesome places of great beauty to express their mood with his subtle melodies. One day when he was fluting at a secluded mountain lake, the daughter of the lake dragon happened to hear his music. Assuming the shape of a huge eel she came to the surface to listen. The sound fascinated her so deeply that she swam close to the shore. Han Hsiang Tsu was amazed to see the unusual fish, and he was even more surprised when he found the eel transforming into a beautiful young lady. Fluting with all his skill he lured her to dry land, but when he paused for a moment the spell was broken and the laughing dragon girl returned to the watery depth.

The next day saw him fluting at the shore once more. His melodies

Han Hsiang Tsu

were no longer expressions of the spirit of the scenery but had become love songs. From dawn to late night he played without rest yet the dragon girl did not return. The next day saw him in emotional turmoil and the day after in despair. He had fallen in love with the dragon princess and would not eat or sleep any longer. Day after day he sought to conjure his love yet no matter how hard he tried, she just would not return to him. Finally in desperation he smashed his flute on the rocks and settled down to die. In the darkest hour of the night he heard movement in the water. It was the eel moving cautiously to the shore. With burning eyes he saw his love rising out of the waves. 'Cry no more', she said, 'You love me as I love you. My father, however, has found out about us and he has kept me locked up. I have barely managed to escape him and have little time. Take this piece of immortal bamboo. It comes from the secret garden of Hsi Wang Mu, where I stole it for you. Make a flute out of it and remember me.' So she handed him the cane and slipped away into the water again.

The stunned lad could hardly hold his tears back. Hsi Wang Mu, the Queen Mother of the West had discovered the theft and she took away the dragon princess to the cave on K'un Lung mountain where she became her handmaiden. Han Hsiang Tsu never managed to meet her again, but when he carved a flute out of the bamboo, its sound healed his heart and enchanted the world. The flute has the power to make flowers grow in an instant and turn people's minds away from suffering. He travelled through the land for centuries until he met Lü Tung Pin who taught him the secret of refining consciousness and he became fully immortal. In the circle of later heaven, Han Hsiang Tsu is represented by the sign Wind, Wood, The Gentle, in the south east. The family name Han can be a reference to the *state of Han* or to *Korea*, to *a star* and to *a fence*. Hsiang can mean *to cook* or a certain *river* that joins the Yangtse in the province of Honan. Tsu is either *a child, heir or son*, or *a master, a sage or an aristocrat*.

Li T'ieh Kuai - Li with the iron crutch is possibly the most popular of the eight immortals, and more stories are told about him than

Li T'ieh Kuai

about any of the others. He began his career as a humble student of the Tao who had retired into the mountain wilderness to enjoy solitude and silence. One day a woodcutter insisted on leaving his daughter at Li's makeshift hut, claiming that the girl wanted to become a nun and hinting at the possibility that she might as well make a good wife. This naturally annoyed young Li who did not feel himself suited to the task of teaching or marrying. Though the daughter did her best to lure him into bed he stoutly refused all advances and remained focused on his meditation. The next day the daughter was gone and when the woodcutter came round to see her, Li was accused of murdering the girl. In spite of all the hollering he remained tranquil and polite, and all of a sudden the woodcutter transformed and revealed that he was no other than old Lao Tsu. The daughter had been but a mirage created to test the sincerity of young Li. Then Lao Tsu taught the young man a number of meditative practices and departed into the otherworld.

During the next years, Li successfully learned the art of leaving his body so that he could fly to the blessed realm where Lao Tsu dwelled. As he grew older he took on a student of his own. Well, one day Li announced to his student that he intended to meet Lao Tsu in the otherworld, and that he wasn't quite certain if he would come back. 'Keep watch and protect my body' he told the student, 'and if I'm not back within seven days you can burn it.' The student promised to fulfill his task dutifully and Li departed, leaving behind a body that soon became cold and rigid. For six long nights the student kept watch. Then he received the bad news that his mother was about to die, and was calling for her only son to come to her death-bed immediately. This placed him in an awful dilemma. To leave his mentor implied a broken vow, but to refuse the wish of his dying mother went against all laws of filial obedience. In a society bound to the rigid code of Confucian ethics, such an act would be one of the worst sins conceivable. After several hours of intense anguish he decided that only a few hours were left to complete the seven days and that his teacher wouldn't return anyway. He set the hut on fire and then hurried to make it to his mother in time.

As you can imagine, Li was somewhat surprised when he came home to his body a little later and found it reduced to a pile of ashes. Who would have thought that the little chat with Lao Tsu had taken so long? Needing a body pretty damn fast he searched the neighborhood, but the only one available happened to belong to a crippled beggar who had died a few hours ago. Li made do with it as he had to. The change from being a healthy young man to a poor outcast cripple turned out to be most enlightening. With his new body he discovered what it is like to be ugly, deformed and loathed. Limping badly, he toured the countryside and found the people cursing him. The dead beggar had been the victim of several disgusting diseases and only with the help of Hsi Wang Mu could they be healed.

In spite of the fact that Lao Tsu's teachings had made him immortal he found that he could produce convincing outbursts of fierce temper, and these turned out to be useful enough when it came to making horrible scenes. Li T'ieh Kuai became the patron of the poor, the outcast and the sick. He walks with the help of an iron crutch and carries a huge gourd bottle that contains all sorts of useful stuff - the medicine of immortality, finest rice wine or the occasional luck giving bat. The gourd bottle is one of the most important Taoist symbols. It can represent the union of heaven and earth and is very handy when a sorcerer wishes to trap an evil demon or wants to cross a river or ocean. While the other immortals can change their appearance completely, Li T'ieh Kuai is always recognizable due to his limping walk. This makes him the natural target of people who think that they can learn the secret of immortality from him. Those who dare to ask may be in for a surprise, as Li has an unusually broad sense of humour. One of them was asked to eat cow manure, another was challenged to follow Li by jumping down a cliff and yet another was offered a pill made from the dirt that the laughing immortal had scratched from his skin. Li T'ieh Kuai can be associated with the sign Li, as it sounds like his name, Fire, The Clinging (there is nothing more clinging than an angry beggar) and the direction south. This suits his temperament. It also relates him to the time of midsummer. On the fifth day of the fifth month, close to the summer solstice, people decorate their doors with paper images of the magical gourd bottle. The family name Li means *plum* and is extremely common in China. T'ieh is *iron* and *firmness*, while Kuai poses the problem that it can mean *to decoy, to swindle* and even *to kidnap* in addition to its possible meaning of *crutch*. The latter is a bit doubtful according to the dictionary.

Ho Hsien Ku generally appears as a beautiful woman. This does not imply that she actually is one, just as the other immortals are not necessarily men. As she pointed out to John Blofeld, to become immortal one has to refine and perfect both the female and the male nature of oneself, and anyway, this self, being originally void and formless, is but an expression of Tao.

In her childhood she accidentally swallowed an immortality conferring potion and henceforth was not interested in worldly pursuits any more. Thus, she caused immense grief to her long-suffering parents by declaring that she would never marry. Such a show of disobedience made her folk decide that she was possessed by a demon. They decided that she was but a useless mouth and set her to do all the housework they could think of.

One day Lü Tung Pin was passing through the village, easy to recognize as an exorcist due to the demon-slaying sword on his back. The parents eagerly invited him to their home, hoping that their deluded daughter would finally be cured of the affliction. Seeing Ho Hsien Ku, he instantly recognized her malady and 'redeemed her' (R. Wilhelm's expression). Together with him she ascended to the sky, and the spoon she had been holding turned into a radiant lotus flower. This flower became her magical symbol, but on some pictures she is also shown with a peach of immortality.

Another noteworthy story, given in more detail by Kwok Man Ho (whose brilliant compilation of tales is highly recommended) claims that she was a humble servant, or more precisely, a slave. The woman of the house used to abuse and beat her whenever she could. One day when her mistress was absent a group of wretched beggars came to the

Ho Hsien Ku

gate and humbly asked for food. Realizing that these outcasts were close to starvation, she dared to give them a little rice. Coming home, the mistress instantly recognized that some rice was missing, and punished poor Ho Hsien Ku for theft. To prove her innocence she offered to recall the beggars, and the lady ordered her to do so. Soon she returned in the company of the poor outcasts. The lady, who enjoyed more power than was good for her, threatened to have the beggars sued and punished unless they immediately vomited every morsel of rice. With a strange glow in their eyes the beggars did so. Then the lady forced Ho Hsien Ku to eat up the vomit, but as soon as she took the first mouthful she found the ground falling away under her. Together with the immortals she flew to heaven and became an immortal herself.

Legend has it that she enjoys to drink, to sing and laugh, but then this also goes for the other seven. In the circle of later heaven her sign is Earth, The Receptive, and her direction is south west. This relates her to the warm season between summer and autumn when the earth brings everything to ripeness. The family name Ho is a character used to pose a question, i.e. *How? Who? What? Why?* etc. Hsien is the word for *immortal* (literally mountain plus human) but also a *fairy* or *elf* or a *cave dweller*. These ideas are closely related. The fairies are often assumed to dwell in caves, just like the immortals are, and these caves are not only in the depths of mountains but also in direct contact with heaven. Ku is a *young woman* or a *girl* or an *aunt on the father's side*.

L ü Tung Pin was a historical person. He was a famous alchemist of the Tang as well as the Sung period. His first birth-date is given as 646 CE. For political reasons he was forced to flee into the desolate mountains where he refined the Tao while living in various caves and grottoes and assumed the name Cave Guest. Numerous Chinese caves are named after him or used to contain shrines dedicated to his worship. As the legends have it, he became an immortal by refining the medicine of metals at an early age. This equipped him with a lot of skill in magick, which is symbolized by his demon-slaying sword and his

Lü Tung Pin

enchanted fly whisk. This unusual object is a common symbol for authority (especially among Chinese Buddhists), a useful tool for spell casting and it also represents his power to fly.

Unlike the other immortals, Lü Tung Pin was still subject to outbursts of uncontrolled temper. It says a lot about him that he failed at the very first academic examination for a comfy government job as the Confucian dogma he was supposed to support made him utterly nauseous. One day when he was flirting with a lady (who was really a flower spirit) her former suitor (a dragon prince) chose to appear and insult the two. In a fit of wrath, Lü Tung Pin hurled his sword after the rival and cut off his head. This overreaction had ill effects on his peace of mind. Before long, Lü Tung Pin lost his tranquillity and became entangled in the world of delusion. He lost his immortality and finally died.

In his next lifetime he achieved a high rank in the government. In spite of his wealth he could not cease from being fascinated by Taoism. One night as he was staying at an inn a charming old man asked to join him for a good cup of warm wine. Lü Tung Pin agreed to this proposal, and while the wine was being warmed he relaxed and happily listened to the old man's soothing voice. Before long his eyes became tired, his lids began to close, and as the old guy droned on, Lü Tung Pin began to dream. The inn faded away and he was on the road once more, heading for the capital of the country. His journey had been a great success! Great honours were showered on him, he was promoted, and as the vision continued he gained great rank and power. Difficult tasks were entrusted to him, and due to his brilliance they were easily mastered. Swift like an arrow he rose on the ladder of rank and as the years flew by he became influential and wealthy and the very emperor himself made Lü Tung Pin his associate and trusted friend.

At the height of his power the emperor happened to die. Bad luck for Lü Tung Pin that the new emperor did not trust him one bit. Soon the former minister was forced to flee the city, leaving his fabulous wealth behind. On the road he learned that his family had been killed by imperial decree and that there was a price on his head. Gone were all former glories. Lü Tung Pin had to assume another name. In poverty and desperation he fled aimlessly across the land, having fallen from absolute power to sheer desolation in a few short days. And having nothing left to lose, he became a hermit and began to refine the Tao.

Somehow this felt strangely familiar to him, as if he had done it once before. With a jolt Lü Tung Pin woke from his slumber. What had seemed like a lifetime to him had been but an instant. The old man, seated on the other side of the table was grinning, and Lü Tung Pin realized that his career as a minister had ended then and there. 'I have given up politics' he said, 'fifty years went by and they were nothing but dross. Henceforth I shall pursue the path of the Tao and attain the priceless treasures of immortality'. This made the old guy laugh. He knew fully well that Lü Tung Pin had just exchanged one ambition for another. 'Meet me in the mountains' he said and disappeared. Lü Tung Pin drank the wine, paid the bill and took the dangerous road into the wilderness. For months he sought to find the old man whose voice just wouldn't fade from his memory. Finally he gave up and settled down in a secluded cave to cultivate the Tao.

One day the old man was back and Lü was delighted. Then the hypnotic voice began to speak again, slowly and irresistibly, and the dreaming began once more. Lu came home and found his entire family dead, all of them having fallen prey to a plague. Calmly he prepared graves but when he put the corpses in their coffins they all woke up and were healthier than before. When he found that he was cheated on the marketplace he laughed and gave away his property to those who had sought to exploit him. Without any belongings, he had to search for herbs to remain alive. Once when he was digging for roots he discovered a great treasure hidden in the earth. Instantly he dug a deeper hole to hide the gold, and shuddered at the thought of the troubles the wealth would have made for any lucky finder. He met a crazy alchemist who claimed to sell the medicine of immortality. Its only snag was that before conferring immortality, the potion was sure to kill. Nobody wanted this doubtful elixir, except for Lü Tung Pin who bought and took it, and found that nothing happened. Dream followed upon dream. Through ten visions the voice of the old man accompanied Lü Tung Pin, and when he finally woke, he was delighted to recognize his old friend Chung Li Chuan sitting in the cave with him. Thus, Lu Tung Pin remembered his own immortality and returned to the company of the blessed.

To this day an immense amount of alchemical Taoist literature is ascribed to the pen of Lü Tung Pin, or Lü Yan as he is sometimes called. This literature is still growing, as he is often invoked in ritual and asked to produce automatic writings. His statue, with sword and whisk is found in plenty of shrines, altars and temples. He is an expert in divination and often consulted for an oracle or a medical prescription. In the circle of later heaven his sign is Lake, The Joyous, which is associated with the direction west, the season of autumn and the energy of metal. This is especially appropriate for a Taoist who supposedly wrote such a lot on the art of distilling metals into the golden pearl. His most famous work is the *Inscription of a Hundred Characters*, which has been treasured and commented by plenty of Taoist adepts.

If you wish to feed the Ch'i forget the words and keep unity. Calm the mind, do by Not-Doing. In activity and rest, know the original source. There is No-Thing; who else do you search? True constancy should answer the people, who answers the people should beware of entanglement. If you refrain from entanglement your nature settles in itself; when your nature is settled the Ch'i returns on its own accord. When the Ch'i returns the elixir comes to be within the cauldron where water and fire are united. Yin and Yang arise and follow each other in unceasing transformation, they sound like thunder everywhere.

White clouds gather around the summit, sweet dew drenches the mountain of the pole, you, yourself, have drunk of the wine of longevity and move freely;

who could recognize you?
    You rest and listen to the sound of the stringless harp (Ch'in) and understand the works of creative change. The sum of these twenty lines is a ladder leading straight to heaven.

His name is full of fascinating meanings and well worth a bit of consideration. The family name Lü can be a reference to *the ancient state of Lü*, but it could also mean a *spine* and a *sword*. Tung is a *cave, hole, grotto*, or a *deep and narrow valley*, reminding you (hopefully) of Lao Tsu's Spirit of the Valley. The character suggests a *fairy cave*, or a cave inhabited by the immortals, but it also refers to the *inner chamber* of a house, this is the sleep-chamber and the place where a marriage is completed and people make love. Pin is a *guest* or a *visitor*.

Lan Ts'ai Ho is one of the most unusual figures in Chinese mythology. According to the *T'ai P'ing Kuang Chi* (978 CE) s/he used to appear on marketplaces, wearing a torn blue robe and only one shoe. The other shoe is either absent or in use as a musical instrument. Lan is the patron of the folk singers and the poets of satirical songs. When s/he chants and sings, s/he likes to use a shoe to hit tables or pieces of wood rhythmically.

To understand Lan you should consider the archetype of the clown or the jester, the person who reverses things, who goes against custom, who makes the thin borderline between sanity and madness hir dwelling place. Lan Ts'ai Ho is outwardly a friendly figure. He or she appears as a beautiful youth or young girl, representing the joy of youth and also its carelessness. To begin with, nobody is really sure if Lan Ts'ai Ho is a young girl or a boy. In some tales s/he appears male, in others female. There is a legend that claims that Lan used to be a singing girl whose songs were anything but entertaining, as they foretold the future. In spite of all desire for prophecy and divination, an overly accurate account of the things that are to come is rarely appreciated.

Lan Ts'ai Ho

The other sort of song that Lan is specialized in - the sort that describes the sum of human toil and effort as vain and useless - is hardly better liked. This does not stop her/him, and mind you, those songs are not only truthful but also very funny. On pictures of the Eight Immortals you can recognize Lan as s/he seems to be the youngest of the group. This is good evidence for the fact that immortality is not reserved for serious alchemists but may also be attained by those who become young and silly. Lan is usually holding a flower basket or a flower pot containing any sort of growth that ever lived on earth. The pot or basket represents pure creative energy. Though it seems to be small enough to be carried easily it contains enough greenery to turn deserts into forests.

Occasionally Lan is also shown with a flute - here is some overlap with Han Hsiang Tsu - or with a gong or a pair of cymbals. When bizarre behaviour is required, Lan is just the person for it. In winter s/he loves to wear thin clothes and in summer thick furs and coats. Laughing at funerals and weeping at birth festivities is another good example. Lan Ts'ai Ho likes to reverse things, a function that threatens the rigid codes of social behaviour. One story claims that s/he heard the true music of heaven one night while drinking in a pub. This is the real music, the music that inspires all the music you can hear and play. Its sound was inaudible to the other drinkers. Lan listened and understood. S/he mounted a passing crane and flew to heaven where s/he became immortal.

In the arrangement of the later heaven, Lan Ts'ai Ho may represent the sign Heaven, The Creative in the north west. This sign corresponds with the season of late autumn or early winter when life hides in the seeds, nuts and grains. The flower basket itself can be seen as such a seed, as it contains all possible future growth and development, and so is Lan, who is young and may yet become anything. The family name Lan is *indigo-blue*, the character includes the symbol for grass and plants. Ts'ai is *to pluck*, originally *to pluck from a tree*, and Ho is *harmony, peace* and a *balanced nature*.

Chang Kuo Lau used to be a white bat, the sort that becomes so old and wise that it can choose to be reborn as a human being. I'm not entirely sure if it is that wise to be born human, but then we need not argue about the matter. One legend says that he first incarnated in the early seventh century as a poor woodcutter. His family soon died and Chang was left with a shabby hut and an ill-tempered donkey. Together with the donkey he used to go into the mountains to cut the wood that was required by the townspeople living in the plains. This life was miserable enough and often for days Chang had to make do with little or no food. One fateful day he chanced to discover a derelict temple hidden in the forest. The donkey, showing more sense than its owner, walked in and Chang, needing a rest in the midday heat, followed the beast. He was amazed that the most mouth-watering scent was coming from the building. Inside, the two discovered a huge cauldron simmering over a bed of coals. The cauldron was full of food! Chang called out but there was no response. Whoever had set up the meal had evidently gone away. 'Well. It's not mine.' Chang said to the donkey. 'I can't steal it, you know.' He sat down in a corner of the building but how could he find rest? He had been hungry for more than a day and the scent simply took his mind away. Cautiously he walked to the pot and looked into it. 'It's quite a lot. Maybe I'll get a bite when its owner comes back. But until then I'll be good and honest and I won't take what doesn't belong to me.' So he sat down again. Then he got up once more. 'I wonder when its owner will come.' The donkey gave him a meaningful look. 'Or do you think that this is a sacrifice for the gods of this place?' The donkey began to grin. 'Maybe the gods might share a little bit with us…stop laughing you donkey!'

Well, the donkey knew what was going on. The food in the cauldron was no ordinary food. The day before a Taoist had found the very herb that confers immortality. To prepare this wort, it has to cook gently for a lengthy period in a sacred space where neither humans nor spirits may find it. The Taoist had prepared the proper mixture and set it up to boil in the ruined temple to make sure that nobody would discover it. Then he had hurried home to look after urgent business, intending

Chang Kuo Lau

to come back secretly after nightfall. What a surprise he had when he came to the temple and found a woodcutter and his donkey, both of them obviously stuffed with food, snoring happily near a cauldron that was just as empty as the great void of the beginning! With a scream of rage the Taoist pulled out a knife. This scream woke Chang who jumped up, and it woke the donkey who began to scream too. Blade gleaming, the Taoist ran for Chang, and Chang in his panic ran for the donkey. With an amazing leap he threw himself on the donkey's back. The donkey had just reversed direction and so Chang happened to land facing the donkey's tail. This was enough for the poor beast. With all its strength the donkey jumped. Chang, holding tight to the tail saw the earth disappearing under him. The donkey who was just as sated with the miraculous food as Chang was, rushed straight to heaven and there the two joined the ranks of the immortals.

Sometimes Chang Kuo Lau folds the donkey up and puts him in his pocket. Then the donkey looks like a simple piece of folded paper. When Chang spits a mouthful of water on it, the donkey reappears in all its former beauty. To this day he rides the donkey facing backwards, and this is quite all right as the donkey usually knows much better where it's going than Chang could.

When you see images of the immortals, you can identify Chang Kuo Lau as an elderly man with a huge beard and any conceivable hat (he wears all sorts). His symbol is a bamboo drum (Yü Ku). This is a piece of thick bamboo that contains two slender rods. When the bamboo is shaken the rods rattle, causing the sort of noise that wakes sleepers and sometimes even the dead. It can be taken as a sign of watchfulness, or of the healthy shock that makes people think differently. More rarely he is shown with a phoenix feather or with a peach of immortality. For some obscure reason he has also become a patron of those who desire children (see Palmer's comments on the subject).

In the later heaven arrangement, Chang Kuo Lau is associated with the sign The Abysmal, Water, corresponding with the direction north and the season of winter. This is the sign of danger, but luckily the donkey, who is as black as the water of the season, has more than enough brains for both of them. It can also spit fire and travel a thousand miles in an instant. There used to be a bronze donkey at the East-Mountain Temple in Peking. Those who touched it on new year's day were healed of their diseases. The place they touched on the donkey had to correspond with their own disease. For mysterious reasons the donkey's genitalia were perfectly polished, though nobody was ever seen touching the statue there. The family name Chang is written with the character *to bend a bow*. Kuo is a *state, land* or *country* while Lau means *old*. The syntax implies that it is not the old country but an elder of a state - provided the name is supposed to make sense and did not accumulate through a series of distortions and misspellings.

T s'ao Kuo Chiu was the uncle of the emperor. He is usually shown as a healthy man of middle age wearing the official clothes and hat required at the court. Another version makes him the younger brother of the Empress Tsao. As a close relation to the regent he enjoyed a number of privileges that were evidently envied by his contemporaries. For one thing, he wore a badge that assured greatest hospitality to its wearer wherever he travelled. When a priest challenged him by pointing out that he was exploiting people who were much poorer, Ts'ao threw the badge into a lake and insisted to pay for food and shelter henceforth.

Ts'ao Kuo Chiu is an interesting figure as he proves that immortality can be gained by all ranks of society, even by those with the poor fortune of being born into the highest rank of society. A legend has it that after the coronation of his sister, Ts'ao and his brothers exploited their new powers mercilessly. Instead of being content with their high rank and the honours that came with it they set up a network of crime and became renowned for greed and cruelty. Indeed the noble brothers did not even refrain from the odd killing, provided it promised enough profit and entertainment. After one such murder, Ts'ao saw sense and decided to give up this lifestyle. While his brothers continued with their ways, Ts'ao left the court and set out to search for the Tao.

Clad in his courtly robes he became the best-dressed hermit in the country. One day as he was meditating in the mountains the immortals came to visit him. 'Isn't he pretty!' said Li with the iron crutch 'Let's test his sincerity!' With an enormous grin he approached Ts'ao and asked 'What is the source of Tao?' This was a trick question of course and Li was just waiting for Ts'ao to commit himself to some ill-chosen answer. Ts'ao, who had learned how to be tricky at the court, smiled politely and pointed to heaven. He did not dare to put his answer into words. This made Li roar with laughter. 'Really? And what is the source of heaven?' Ts'ao pointed at his own heart (i.e. the seat of mind and awareness). Seeing the reply the immortals laughed so much that they rolled on the ground in their hilarity. They took him along nevertheless and so Ts'ao Kuo Chiu became immortal as well.

In pictures he is usually equipped with a pair of wooden click sticks or a pair of castanets. You can often hear such instruments in the ritual music of ceremonial Taoism. They have a sharp and overtone rich sound that has an almost shattering effect on the minds of the listeners. Like so many ritual instruments they do not necessarily sound pleasing. It's their function to mark time and intervals in the ceremony and to wake those who dream or get carried away. There is also something really ancient to the sound, as no doubt people used to beat sticks against each other long before the more refined instruments were invented.

Occasionally Ts'ao is shown holding a courtly sceptre, but don't ask me what he is supposed to do with it. Having lived at the court for a long time he became an adept in the art of deception, and maybe he was adopted as the patron of actors for this reason. In the chart of later heaven he may represent the sign Keeping Still, Mountain in the north east. This corresponds with the season when winter fades but spring has not yet arrived. By keeping still and voiding his heart, Ts'ao represents the sage who may sit in the center of the court without noticing anything. The family name Ts'ao means *statesman* or *official*, in Kuo you can recognize the term *state, land, country* while Chiu is an *uncle on the mothers side*, a hint at his aristocratic family.

Ts'ao Kuo Chiu

This closes the circle and brings us to the beginning. As you can see the Eight Immortals can represent the eight magickal kua. Though they probably only became a group during the last couple of centuries, it may be that their harmony with the eight signs is a key to their common appearance. Their individual nature is an expression of Tao, but this expression in turn requires a group that is so well balanced and harmonious that one might almost call it a group sentience.

Many images of them show them travelling to the Western Paradise where Hsi Wang Mu guards the secret potions that confer immortality. On their way they have to cross a stream that consists of such soft water that nothing can float on it. Seven immortals cross it by floating on the leaves of an enchanted lotus flower or on Li's powerful gourd while Lü Tung Pin flies across the river that divides the worlds with the aid of his fly whisk. In her splendid cave in the K'un lun mountains Hsi Wang Mu sits on a throne that combines the energies of the green dragon of the east and the white tiger of the west. In front of her a pair of hares are crushing the sacred herbs and long-stalked mushrooms in a mortar, the toad of the moon plays with the raven of the sun (each of them recognizable due to the fact that it has three legs), and the nine-tailed fox dances to the sound of Hsi Wang Mu's superb whistling and fluting.

The sacred mountains themselves are the place where the cosmic axis connects the pole star of heaven with the world and with the underworldly yellow springs (the place of death and dissolution). From the top of the highest peaks a sacred 'Tree of Life' rises into the stellar splendour of heaven, a vision that is closely related to mythologies of several 'shamanic' Eurasian cultures. Here is the strange and forgotten land of Mu which can't be found on any map. The mountains are in the center of everything, and in their caves and caverns you can find the immortals drinking and laughing and singing silly songs. The deepest caves connect with the height of heaven. You can find the Immortals exploring the hidden delights of enchanted fairy grottoes, flower gardens, pine forests and pleasant autumn lakes. They walk on clouds, they sit in shady valleys enjoying the swirling mists and rest in the heart of the living midnight. You can meet them in the centre of yourself once you become empty enough. And you can meet them out here, walking in the world, disguised as mortals. They often assume physical form to manifest on earth. Then they live, and do their work, and celebrate, and finally they return to the Western Paradise until the time for incarnation comes once more. Take a good look around when you go about your business. It could be that there are immortals in your neighbourhood! Maybe the laughing beggar at the street-corner is an immortal, or the traveller on the road, the artisan or scholar, the official or the lunatic. Maybe you should take a deep look into a mirror. Who knows if you will recognize an immortal hiding right behind your face?

Hsi Wang Mu

Appendix Two
Refining Vapours

One of the specialties of Taoist magic and meditation is the use of colours. Colours abound in Chinese folk ritual, in the realm of the spirits and in the various otherworldly realms. Consider traditional Chinese theatre for example. An actor with a bright red or purple face is not necessarily a monster or suffering from a heart or skin disease. These colours signify loyalty and a tranquil spirit. A blue face can signify the god of literature, or the king of demons. It can also hint that a certain character has a nasty personality or is a ghost. Actors with black faces are rough but honest. (Eberhard). Various Taoist sects wear different ritual garments. You can recognize a member of the southern monastic orders as they wear white robes with square hats. The Ch'üan Chen Sect prefers a black robe with a fish hat, while the Cheng-I Taoists dress in red robes and replace the ceremonial hat with a golden crown.

Basic to the colour code of ritual meditation and magic are the colours of the five movers. For such practices, the colours are usually visualized as mist, fog, steam, clouds and occasionally rain. Taoist literature tends to use the term 'vapour' for such concepts. A vapour, mist or haze has enough form to be visualized, but not enough to limit the Taoist to a specific shape. You can find the green-blue vapour of wood/wind in the east, where it assumes the form of an azure dragon. In the body, this vapour is usually stored in the liver. South offers the red vapour of fire, symbolized by a phoenix, a red raven or a fiery pheasant. In the body, this vapour is stored in the heart. In the west arises the white vapour of metal/precious stones, its power beast is the white snow tiger, and its location in the body is in the lungs. North offers the cold, black vapour of water, its animal is usually a tortoise (the black warrior), a snake or both of them entwined. The black vapour has its seat in the kidneys. Finally, in the center you can encounter the yellow vapour of earth, its storage space is the spleen.

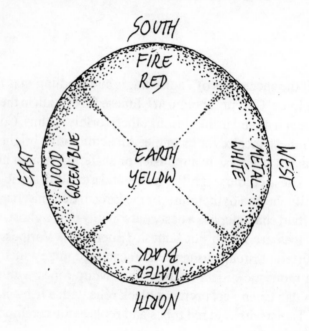

This system offers five basic colours and combines them with the directions, with animals, and with organs of the body. It can be extended indefinitely, as you probably expected, by assigning the five mythical emperors to the directions (there seem to be several ways of doing this), the five sacred mountains, the five noxious beasts and whatever else can be reduced to a five-fold symmetry. One good example is the lunar houses. These correspond with twenty-eight constellations, each of them guarded by an animal spirit. The twenty-eight constellations are in turn ordered by colours and moving energies, as you can see in this list:

Wood	blue/green:	rain-dragon, unicorn, wolf, wild dog.

Metal	white:	dragon, ox, domesticated dog, sheep/goat.

Earth	yellow:	badger, bat, ring-necked pheasant, roebuck.

Sun	red:	rabbit, rat, cock, horse.

Moon	deep blue:	fox, swallow, crow, stag.

Fire	crimson:	tiger, pig, monkey, snake.

Water	black:	leopard, snail, ape, earthworm.

This list follows the invaluable study of Michael Saso. Another system of attribution given by Kermadec (after Havret and Chambeau, Shanghai 1922) goes as follows:

Wood	green/blue:	crocodile, dragon, badger, hare, fox, tiger, leopard.

Water	black:	unicorn, ox, bat, rat, swallow, pig, porcupine(?).

Metal	white:	wolf, dog, pheasant, cock, raven, ape, gibbon.

Fire earth	red:	tapir, goat, fallow deer, horse, deer, serpent, worm.

Though these lists are not fully in accord with each other they may still be of use for your meditation. You can learn how the ancient astronomers thought of the five movers by contemplating the nature, appearance and behaviour of the animals that symbolize them. Visualize the coloured energies, project an animal into the colour and find out what they have in common. Of course this exercise ought to be done in an easygoing way. It may be worth considering that the symbolic animals are not quite the same as real animals, and that the five movers are not necessarily identical with the substances chosen to represent them. Taoist cosmology is a very fluid art, as its symbols are meant to suggest meaning, not to define it.

The three fives

One of the key concepts of early alchemical literature is to blend and refine the three fives. In the classic handbook of inner alchemy, the *Cantong Qi*, or *Triplex Unity* by Wei Boyang (c. 142 CE, Eastern Han Dynasty) this concept is already fully developed: *If the three fives have never been joined, hard and soft remain separate. (...) The three fives combine to become whole, this is the seed of heaven and earth.* What then are the three fives that they have such an important role in the refining of the Taoist adept? The answer comes from a combination of numerology with the meditation called 'Fasting the Heart'. Look at the chart that Fu Hsi discovered on the dragon horse rising from the river. Each of its directions is symbolized by numbers. Thus you have black water in the north, signifying the number one. Fire is number two, wood is number three, metal is number four and earth, the center, is number five. It is from the numbers of the movers that you can unite the three fives. This process is part of the Tsao-Ch'ao meditation.

As you may recall, the Taoist story of creation states that out of the Hun Tun, the primal polarity of yin and yang appeared. Then yin and yang developed the three levels, out of these arose the five movers, and these are the root of the ten-thousand things that clutter up the universe. As the Taoist is primarily interested in joining with the flow of Tao, and Tao generally appears only in a void mind, the main aim of this meditation is to reverse the flow of creation, to return to the primal chaos of the Hun Tun.

The ritual meditation begins with the first five. The Taoist evokes the green vapour of wood/wind and the red vapour of fire. Wood is

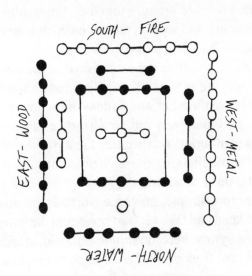

Map of the River Ho

three, fire is two, and when they unite we reach the first five. The two vapours are drawn into the body and refined in the empty center of the microcosmos, the so-called yellow court. The vapours of green and red blend and form a vapour that is green blue. This is not what happens when you mix water-colours, but then those early sages did not really bother about what occurs to painters who take alchemical instructions literally.

Anyway, the first five is a green/blue vapour. It is called 'Primordial Breath' and rises to the head. Within the head, it becomes the dwelling of Yüan-Shih T'ien-Tsun, the Primordial Heaven Worthy, who may be a personification (if this is possible) of the Hun Tun.

The second five is a single vapour. This is the vapour of earth (the number of earth is five), a yellow mist which is drawn into the body and congealed around the heart. This site houses the Ling Pao Heavenly Worthy who dwells between heaven and earth in a yellow/golden haze.

The third five comes from the union of white vapour (metal,

number four) and black vapour, corresponding with water and number one. When these two are brought together, the result is not grey, as it would be in painting, but a white radiance which is stored in the lower belly, housing the Tao-Te Heavenly Worthy.

When the three worthies are established in the three levels of the body, the vapours are moved. In this visualization, the white vapour moves to the back of the head, and so does the yellow/golden haze. The two mix with the blue/green vapour already established in the head, and then all three mingle directly under the top of the skull. As you can see, during the meditation, the alchemist has simplified the five movers into the three worthies.

To become more simple, the three worthies are now exteriorized. They leave the head and take seats of honour in the temple, leaving the Taoist, who has by now become simple and void, to unite with the Hun Tun and to join the flow of the Tao. This is not all there is to the rite, as there exist several versions of it, each of them complicated by various gestures, sacred words and whatnot, but even without these, you should be able to discern the basic structure and invent some way of adapting it to your own requirements.

The ability to perform such meditative rituals of attaining emptiness is one of the issues that settles the rank of a Taoist. This issue is also what distinguishes orthodox (Cheng) and heterodox (Hsieh) Taoists. Generally speaking, and oversimplifying the issue as usual, an orthodox Taoist is primarily concerned with rituals that produce union with the Tao and offer healing and blessing to the community. A heterodox Taoist, on the other hand, may well be more interested in popular rituals, in performing ceremonies, and may possibly make a good living from selling sorceries, talismans and bewitchment. This distinction is somewhat misleading however, as the criteria for who does what are not that perfectly worked out. If a Taoist follows the time-honoured traditions precisely, this makes her/him an orthodox Taoist. If you subscribe to this point of view, only very few practitioners might be called orthodox. Most Taoist sects did have the odd innovation from time to time, and from the traditionalist point of view, they are all heterodox, and in error. Sects that introduced new colour codes, spirits, sacred words, hand-gestures and so on became instantly suspect in the eyes of the orthodox practitioners, who insisted that such delusions cannot produce real magic nor real union with the Tao, whatever that may mean.

Others use the terms more loosely, i.e. orthodox Taoists are members of their own group while the heterodox bunch consists of anybody else. Taoist thought is not very tolerant regarding these issues, and such injunctions as *Uphold the orthodox, dispel the heterodox* occur with some frequency in Taoist rituals. Thus, if you improve on these rituals or make use of your own associations with regard to colours, spirits, symbols and the like, you have to accept that most Taoists would call you heterodox and frown mightily. On the other hand, magick is a very pragmatic science, and one of its essentials is the attitude of making use of what works. If only the orthodox traditionalist school had the right methods, the countless heterodox sects would never have come to exist. Each heterodox cult was founded on the insights and inspiration of people who dared to be original, and who preferred to use what suited them, as it usually worked a lot better. Their followers, in turn, forgot all about originality and made the new system another orthodoxy until some daring soul innovated it once more.

In fact, each orthodoxy began as a heterodox, revolutionary system, and if you think about it you may discover that the only lasting tradition is one of constant innovation. This may not suit a lot of self-important priests but it does suit the changeful flow of the Tao.

The colourful vapours have come to play an important part of Taoist magic. As was mentioned earlier, a black vapour can signify water and put to use to make rain. If it comes from the invisible stars of the northern sky, it can also be applied to render the adept invisible. Thus, a black vapour can signify water or the invisible stars, but this does not mean that water and the dark stars are identical. This is one of the joys of Taoist literature and mysticism. There are hundreds of metaphors in use, and most of them are not quite specific. What a given metaphor may mean depends mainly on the context and the degree of insight expected from the practitioner. The green/blue vapour that houses the Primordial Heavenly Worthy in the head is not identical with the green/blue energy of wood/wind, though they have some aspects in common.

In some texts the energy of wood is green, in others blue, or a turquoise mixture of the two. What precisely stimulates your mind with wood energy is yet another question. Which shade of green makes wood/wind come to life for you? There is a lot of difference between the fresh green of young leaves in spring, the darker greens you encounter when you rest among evergreens, or the more brownish greens that turn up at the end of summer. Each of them produces a distinct mood, energy and consciousness. I suggest you visualize the vapours and find out which precise colours work for you. If you rely on the colour code as given by various adepts, you have to accept that they will only work efficently for you if you are really similar to them. If you are not, and this is what life is all about, you will have to discover what turns you on.

The colours are often used in alchemical literature. Sometimes they may refer to the five movers, sometimes to the eight trigrams, and sometimes to entirely different phenomena. Alchemical literature makes much of the trigrams Kan (Water, The Abysmal) and Li (Fire, The Clinging). Generally, Kan may refer to the Ch'i as it flows down (water descends), and Li to the rising of the Ch'i (fire ascends). They can also represent lead and mercury, or deep mind and conscious attention, and alot of other forces and ideas. In essence, Kan and Li circulate in the body, their passage representing the Round Way of Heaven.

The signs Kan and Li may be called the black and the white, or the subtle pearl and the golden blossom. This does not accord with the classical *Shuogua* commentary to the *I Ching*, which calls Kan blood-red and fails to provide a colour for Li. It associates the colour black with the trigram Kun and white with the sign Sun. If you insist on a single interpretation you won't get anywhere.

The interaction of Kan and Li produces the panacea, the medicine that cures all ills. Common metaphors for this consciousness are *the union of tiger and dragon* (this implies white and green), *the tortoise and the snake as they embrace* (they are both black according to most colour codes), *dark and yellow forming a design, metal and earth mingling* (white and yellow), *red and black acting in harmony* and *mingled red and white*.

The easiest way to misunderstand such expressions is to take them literally. As Yuyan (1284 CE) commented: *Whatever you may call it, it is nothing but spirit (xin) and breath which combine to form a whole (...) When breath has calmed the inner energy congeals and the Inner Elixir can form. This requires no massage and no breathing techniques, and it is not necessary to manipulate thought.* This may sound almost too simple. Maybe the early alchemists invented all those flowery titles in order to make people think. When something seems too simple, few people bother to contemplate it in depth.

Or consider the titles given to what may be called *the original spirit* (yuanshen). The original spirit is a key concept in Taoism. The original spirit is our original consciousness, is the self that exists before birth and after death, is the timeless harmony of the primal heaven. Yuyan, for the fun of it, lists more than seventy metaphors for this idea. Several of them are colourful, or imply specific colours. *The palace of jade-purity, the jade-cauldron, the jade-hall, the jade-room, the jade-canopy* may all be assigned to colours ranging from green to white, as these are the usual colours of jade.

Jade, as a sacred substance was often used as a metaphor for the height of heaven and was thought to preserve and extend life. *The saint wears simple clothes - but within, he wears jade. Tao Te Ching,* Chapter 35 (70). Green also appears in the terms *the ancient forest* and *the ancient hill.* Just as popular was a reference involving purple or violet. These colours are especially interesting as they are not included in the usual range of the five movers. *The purple barn, the purple court, the purple wall* and *the purple-golden cauldron* are good examples. Red is only obvious in one title, *the cauldron of red sand,* while *the cauldron of mercury* implies silver or grey.

Invisible colours occur more often: *the highest invisible palace, the highest hidden gate, the hidden palace, the hidden room, the hidden field.* Darkness occurs in the titles *the dark city* and *the honoured darkness*, and brown is implied by *the honoured pot of earth* and by the popular *palace of the mud-ball*, which is a term for the brain. Add to these *the highest peak, the precious peak, the blessed majestic peak, the height of Mount K'un lun* and we come to the colours as they appear in the realm of the immortals.

I have already mentioned the goddess Hsi Wang Mu, and the way she used to function as a deity concerned with death, the otherworld and immortality during the Han dynasty and earlier. In later periods her function changed considerably. She was transformed into a bizarre mother-goddess with countless semi-divine daughters and only one son.

Likewise, the K'un Lun mountains transformed into a realm of pure paradise where the immortals go to celebrate. A comparatively late rendering of this idea divides her realm as follows. K'un Lun, the highest peaks in the world, are divided from common reality by a broad stream of soft water on which nothing can float. Next one comes upon a wall of terrifying height. This wall is red and it is composed of precious stones. Comparing these precious stones with the jewels selected by Nü Kua to repair the pillar of heaven it might be an idea that each of them is conscious and represents an individual dedicated to the cult. This is just speculation of course, though it may make some sense to those who have enjoyed *The Dream of the Red Chamber*. Between the mountain itself and the wall lies a realm housing immortals. On the right wing, close to the kingfisher-brook, you can find the male immortals. On the left wing the female immortals dwell, who are thought to dress in colours to express their function: red, blue, black, violet, yellow, green, and natural (nude?). It is Hsi Wang Mu herself who supplies the important golden colour that symbolizes the primal consciousness, the elixir of immortality. In this aspect she is known as Chin Mu, which may be translated as golden, or precious lady (or mother). (see Funk and Wagnall's *Standard Dictionary of Folklore, Mythology and Legend*).

As the golden lady she is also known as the Metal Mother, closely associated with the alchemical art of transforming base substances into the golden blossom of immortal consciousness.

Other interesting colours associated with her cult appear in the Yellow Springs beneath Mount K'un Lun (the place of death and dissolution), in the famed jade lake close to the summit of the mountain and the huge peaches growing in her orchards. These peaches grow to miraculous taste and size and grant immortality to all who partake of them. Every couple of thousand years the goddess invites all deities, spirits and immortals to join her peach-banquet in the Hall of Azure Jade, an event satirized in the magnificent novel *The Journey to the West*.

What makes Mount K'un Lun so important for Taoist alchemy is the fact that this highest mountain of the world is not to be found on any map. At first glance it would be easy to speculate that Hsi Wang Mu, as a lady of the west, dwells in the Himalayas. This may have been so for a period in earliest pre-history, but generally, Chinese geographers knew about the Himalayas, and decided that these were not K'un Lun. Consider that there is evidence for Chinese silk being traded all the way to Southern Germany where it came to rest in the barrow of a Celtic noble (at Hochdorf near Stuttgart). If traders linked the Chinese and the Celtic people in the centuries before the common era, it is likely that they were aware that the K'un Lun mountain with all its magical attributes did not exist anywhere in-between.

The highest mountains were always assumed to be a bit beyond the known realm, just beyond the western horizon, where the sun goes down in orange, peach and amber beauty. To reach those mountains of paradise, the traveller has to pass through the land of death. Some alchemical texts identify the nine levels of Mount K'un Lun with the human spine, thus, the peak of the mountain corresponds with the crown of the head, but of course such insights never made it into common folklore as they are simply too subtle. The description of

Mount K'un Lun parallels a description of the body/mind complex of an immortal adept, the geographical map being also a map of primal consciousness. Within the mountain you can find the eight grottoes of the immortals. The number eight may remind you of the eight signs, the Pa Kua, and their arrangement in circles. Indeed the process of alchemical refinement necessitates a shift from the map of later heaven (the temporal world) to the map of primal heaven, representing the timeless and eternal realm, and the self that exists beyond the dream of life and death.

Exploring yourself

But let us now turn from the land of the otherworldly ones to the topic of actual practise. What can be done with the colourful vapours? There are plenty of answers to this question. Let me offer some suggestions and ask you to invent some uses for yourself.

To begin with, it can be useful to visualize the body as a microcosmos. Within it, the sacred energies move. They rise, so Yuyan tells us, like the fog and mists rising from the sides of a mountain into empty space. Like falling rain they descend, and like the floods of spring they wash through the mind/body system. The energies come and go, and when the mind is empty and silent, they blend and form the sacred elixir.

A common activity in Taoist ritual involves the refinement of colourful vapours within the alchemical oven of the body. During various stages of ritual, the Taoist presses a finger-joint, faces a certain direction of the circle, sees a vapour arise and draws it into the body. Then the vapour is circulated, mixed with the bodies own triple vapours, and centered in the yellow court. This basic procedure is used for a number of magical activities.

When such a vapour is properly prepared, it can be expelled while a sigil is drawn. This act gives potency to the sigil and makes it valid in the eyes of the spirits. In a similar fashion, a special vapour may be distilled to consecrate a talisman or to exorcise an evil spirit. A healing breath may be blown at a suffering patient, or a ritual space may be charged with subtle energies.

As can be expected, there are plenty of refining complications involved in such procedures, each Taoist sect having developed a range of its own which is absolutely certain to work miracles. In actual practise you may as well consider what you need to fit this method with your own way of magick, and how to refine it for further and better uses. For these purposes, a number of further vapours are available.

A solar vapour can be derived from the seven rayed sun which shines above the corner of the left eye while a lunar vapour may be drawn from the full moon disk which shines from the corner of the Taoists right eye. In my experience, three of the most interesting breaths come in the colours green, amber and purple. As mentioned before, the names of these colours are only crude guidelines to tell you in which direction to search. You will get different results from different shades of these colours, the vital question being what makes the proper energies come to life for you.

For a start it might be useful to become a bit more colour conscious. Go for a walk in the forest and take a good look at all the greens you can find. Fresh green of young leaves, deeper hues of older foliage, the shady colours of spruce and pine and fir, dark olive, mosses, lichen, ferns swaying at the sides of hidden waterways...all of them offer distinct tones of green, options of greenishness that have distinct effects on your mind.

Next, draw attention to the inner world and imagine greens. Which greens excite you? Which greens soothe? What would be a nice toxic green, and what the proper shade to remind you of the primal forest? Think of the Green Emperor Fu Hsi, who invented the eight signs and aligned them in his spiderweb, the circle of primal heaven. This was at the very beginning, long before the advent of agriculture, in the ancient forest of the dawn ages. Which greens would suit the primal wildwood, the ancestral country that gave birth to human sentience? As you invent greens and explore their effects on your mind you will learn that there are several shades or mixtures of green that have profound effects on you.

Now one of the advantages of the idea of vapours is that a vapour is of a highly subtle, changeful nature. Vapours, smoke, clouds and fumes exist between form and absence. They have enough substance to be imagined but not so much that it ties them to specific forms or standards. When you visualize the motion of a green vapour, this vapour can include many shades of colouration, it can change indefinitely and include a wide range of options. This is highly useful as it prevents the imagination from becoming too dull.

The amber range includes a similar wealth of options. When you mix yellow with red you can produce a lot of colours, such as orange, peach, amber, ochre, and include gold, for completeness. Think of the colours of the autumn forest, the splendour of the sky at sunrise and sunset, and go out to enjoy them in the wild, as the immortals used to do. How many shades can you discover in nature? How many can you discover right within your mind?

More subtle is the purple range. There are plenty of different degrees between red and blue. Think of the fresh colour of pale lilac, of mauve, aubergine, lavender, heather in bloom, of the hidden colours of fog, of snow in the twilight forest, of the nightsky at the fading of the sunset. Look for them in nature and in your own mind and find out what turns you on.

You may notice that green, orange and purple all convey a distinct quality of in-between-ness, of a sentience that exists somewhere beyond the ordinary range of perception. This may be one of the reasons why the original consciousness is often associated with these colours, be it as the jade heights of the highest heaven, the purple twilight of the pre-manifest or the peach banquet that conveys immortality and transcendence of flesh and personality. Such vapours were rarely used for everyday magic but had their use for certain subtle transformations.

One phenomenon that occurs quite frequently in Chinese literature is the appearance or departure of a deity or an immortal on clouds and vapours. The art of riding on clouds has been the goal of many Taoist adepts. A fascinating text entitled *The Lord of the Golden Tower of the High Pure Realm's Illustrated Instructions on (Visualizing) the Five Bushels and the Three Ones* contains detailed instructions on the art of flying to the stars. First, the Taoist is advised to sit facing east at midnight of the spring equinox. This may be a reference to a specific time, but more likely is a reference to a state of mind. Alchemical literature, starting with Wei Boyang, is full of such dates and times, and woe to the Taoist who takes them literally. Midnight is not necessarily a time of day but a consciousness, symbolized by the trigrams Kun or Kan, representing the instant when from utter darkness (primal heaven) and danger (later heaven) the seed of fresh light (and life) is born. This is the Living Midnight, the birth of the golden elixir, the darkness of new moon when sun (Li) and moon (Kan) unite to bring forth the primal awareness, to use but a few flowery metaphors for an event that necessarily defies description.

Sorry if this may sound like an awfully complicated matter when it is really so simple that I have no words for it. At this hour the adept is advised to keep her/his guardian deity within, along with the three palaces, the three officials and the three ones. If you have come this far you should be able to guess at the meaning of these, or invent your own.

Next, the Taoist is asked to *ride the smoke of the purple vapor and step up to the Northern Bushel's (Big Dipper's) Bright Star. The Bright Daylight Star is the Eastern Deity of the Bushel. In this way you will be transported to the center of the stars. Sit and inhale the purple vapor thirty times. Soon you will see the Eastern High Palace of the Bright Daylight Star. Inside the Palace is the Child of the Green Mystery who will give you the True Light.* (transl. Eva Wong). It may be interesting to consider that this method of attainment also includes a subtle allusion to death. The Big Dipper, appearing so prominently in all sorts of rituals, is also the dark deity of death in Chinese lore. Again, the way to immortality goes through the gates of personal dissolution, just as the realm of the immortals in the west is actually an otherworldly realm reached by those who have left body and personality behind. An immortal consciousness is impossible for those who cling to life and those who ask Hsi Wang Mu for the golden elixir are devoured and get exactly what they asked for. Wei Boyang may have alluded to this mysterious transformation when he wrote the enigmatic lines *thus body dies, the soul disappears. Then the colour turns to deepest purple, shining and radiant appears the transformed elixir.* Purple colour can be associated with sorrow and sadness, but it is also associated with the highest heaven.

Should you like to experiment with the subtle vapours it may be of use to add a few practical hints. For a start, it is useful to calm down, relax and soothe the mind before evoking any vapour. Observing the flow of breath, as it becomes soft and smooth, is highly recommended. Alchemical literature calls this process *tuning the breath* or *sending attention into the cave of breath.* It is one of the essential acts of meditation. To make the breath smooth, however, is not active doing but achieved in its own good time by not-doing, by allowing breath to return to natural simplicity. As breath becomes calm and smooth, so does awareness, and eventually both may be forgotten. As you will realize, this is not a breathing technique. In fact it is an attitude that does without any technique, and any intent or effort. Some texts call it the true breath, of which Ho Hsien Ku said *The stem of life is in the true breath.* (Cleary 1996).

When you begin to visualize vapours you have several choices. You can imagine a vapour outside of yourself, and draw it into your body. You can imagine it within yourself, as it circulates. You can surround yourself with the vapour, and allow it to saturate you. You can store it in your body, and find out how different storage spaces influence your consciousness. In these issues, it may be useful to consider that the distinction between outside and inside is somewhat arbitrary. Both the outer and the inner universe are thoughts of the mind, and this mind has no place and is no thing. Consequently, the important issue is that you find out what happens.

You may find that certain vapours, and certain ways of visualizing them can change your awareness. Keep in mind that the vapours are not things in themselves but representations of more primal energies and sentiences. Yuyan pointed out that an alignment of the unborn inner energies (primal heaven) and the manifest outer energies (later heaven) produces a state as if the practitioner were slightly drunk. He did not specify how exactly this happened to him, but it is worth considering that such changes of awareness are not only possible but also natural. The Eight Immortals, for instance, are known to be drunk quite frequently, and it is not likely that anything as crude as alcohol is involved in their festivities. I can't tell you how to work this transformation, but with a bit of experiment, you can. When you align the coloured vapours with your true breath, you may be in for several of surprises. One useful attitude to keep in mind is to allow the breath to stay smooth and natural. Even if you use breath to project a vapour into a talisman, a sigil or apply it to banish an unwanted influence (such as the desires and fears of your ego), it is sound practise to keep it gentle and tranquil. Violent exhalation may be of use for public ritual or dramatic play-acting, but it involves the risk that your mind is upset and the trance is disturbed. It can be used on occasion, but a serene breath is usually more efficient. Whether you exhale a vapour out of mouth or nostrils is your own choice as both methods are used in Taoist magic. The vapours may be gates that lead your attention on a journey to yourself. Once you arrive you may find that you have always been there, give a laugh, and go beyond.

Some notes on the illustrations

A Chinese proverb tells us that a picture says more than a thousand words. Hypnotherapy, on the other hand, gives good evidence that a single word can produce a thousand pictures, especially if it is a vague term inviting the hearer to hallucinate. What could be more easy to understand than a book with pictures? As I recently learned there do happen to be people around who can't make sense of pictures or words. Luckily they are rare, few and in-between. Some of them can't see sense as they have decided to consider themselves artists, while others distrust a playful approach to serious scholarly matters. As the pictures for this book accumulated I realized that they constitute such a mixture of historic items and personal visions that some of my more interested readers might like to learn more about the background they developed out of. Let me name a few and give a few short comments.

The picture of the death of the Hun Tun is based loosely on Chuang Tsu's account. In my vision, the forces of light and darkness assumed the forms of screeching carrion birds. This is a personal interpretation and has no foundation in Chinese myth. It might remind you, however, that yin and yang are not necessarily nice or sacred, even if their intentions are friendly. In the story they create the world of illusion by slaying the primal chaos.

The image of Fu Hsi and Nü Kua, both of them with serpent tails, comes from a large stone picture. The original is in the temple of Wuliang in the province of Shandong. Its not improved or edited but a simple to scale representation in black and white (after Eberhard). I leave the question of who is who on this image to you.

In the picture of Fu Hsi, the Green Emperor holds the standard form of the circle of primal heaven in his hands. This is the most popular version and is based on the classic *Shuogua* commentary. In the elder Mawangdui version, the text is somewhat different, and accordingly, the order of the hexagrams suggests a different chart of early heaven. The interested reader might enjoy to draw this version and contemplate its meaning. Chien in the South, Ken in the S/E, Kan in the East, Chen in the N/E, Kun in the North, Tui in the N/W, Li in the West and Sun in the S/W. This pattern gives the order of the top trigrams as they appear in the Mawangdui *I Ching*. The organization of this circle is very regular and more symmetrical than the picture of primal heaven that is usually given. Note that the circle neatly divides into two halves, one of them with a single yin, one with a single yang line. The bottom trigrams of Mawangdui are ordered in a pattern that is based on this list: Chien S, Kun S/E, Ken E, Tui N/E, Kan N, Li N/W, Chen W, Sun S/W. As you can see, the second list has each trigram followed by the one that opposes it in the top version, ie they appear as pairs. Keep in mind that some authors, such as Wei Boyang, used the image of primal heaven to hint cautiously at the circulation of Ch'i within the body. To understand this, consider that in each tri- and hexagram, motion occurs from bottom to the top. The beginning of this process is usually the sign Kun in the north which is totally dark and passive (the living midnight, hence new moon and death) and the instant of absence out of which the first yang, the golden elixir is born. This works with the usual layout, but even better with the Mawangdui version. Nevertheless, the first sign born out of Kun is Chen.

The turtle rising out of the water refers to the vision that Yü the

Great had when he walked on the riverbank and pondered how to control the great flood. While later periods identified the tortoise with the direction north and the moving force of dark water and winter, earlier Chinese traditions identify the world itself with a tortoise. When Nü Kua ordered the world in the beginning, she took the legs of a gigantic tortoise and fashioned the four pillars that support the sky out of them. These legs symbolize the directions and the order of the world. You can see the origin for divination by means of turtle shells and shoulder bones in the vision that Yü had at the banks of the great stream. Unlike the picture of the turtle, which is based on Chinese paintings, the oracle of the Shang period (16-11th century BCE) generally made use of the turtle's belly armor. In a special pit (Anyang, province Henan) archaeologists discovered 1558 fragments of turtle shells, 579 of them with inscriptions. These lots had holes drilled into them, to make it more easy for fire to crack them, and often showed inscriptions in an early script telling us the questions asked and the answers received from the oracle. Several shells had a large hole at a side, so they may have been bound by a piece of string. This places these shells among the oldest books of humanity. Sadly, the inscriptions are often somewhat boring. Favourite topics are the success of nobles going out to hunt boar and other beasts, weather and harvest, the health of regents, the chances for victory in battle and the amount of people and beasts that were to be sacrificed to ensure the blessing of the gods. Didn't these diviners have anything more interesting to ask?

The Liubo gameboard is from the royal tombs of Zhongshan, district Hebei. It dates from the period of the warring kingdoms, sometime between 481-222 BCE.

The strangely zoomorphic figure was included as it reminds me of a person riding a bear, or a bear-human transformation. This is just guesswork of course. It comes from the side of a ritual jade vessel (cong) of the Liangzhu culture, c. 3000-2800 BCE, found in Fanshan, district Zhejiang.

The picture of the serpent with the trigrams is based on an

illustration found in Michael Saso's excellent study.

The pair of good-luck bats is based on a Chinese design.

Lao Tsu on the water buffalo is a pretty traditional representation of the old sage. While busy writing this book, I dreamed how to draw this picture. It was basically a question of the point of view. The Lao Tsu riding the buffalo is about to depart from the known world - civilized China - into the mysterious and dangerous west. This could mean a journey into death, into the sunset, to India or the Himalayas, into some unknown otherworld or into the western paradise where the immortals find their recreation. How do you show this journey? In the dream I moved around the rider and watched the migration from several angles, from in front, above, the sides, below and so on. It was amazing how the meaning of the picture changed with each new perspective. If you feel like learning something useful, give this a try. Imagine the old boy on his huge black buffalo from all sorts of perspectives and distances. When you've observed the event from a dozen angles you'll have learned something about the meaning that your mind supplies for any given point of view. Then do this with another picture. Find out what sort of reaction you produce when seeing things from various perspectives, and make use of this knowledge to improve your visualization. Anyway, after settling the Lao Tsu picture (this involved some subsequent visits to farms in order to have a good look at the form of cow bums. Apologies to all water-buffalo enthusiasts - there are none around here and so the picture is a bit on the imaginative side) the next image dreamed was the picture of Chuang Tsu and the butterfly. The dream settled that the most useful approach was the butterfly perspective. The face you see on the picture is loosely based on Tseng Kuo Fan's portrait, (the beard was too good to be ignored), but my picture is kinder. The original has the old sage wearing something that looks suspiciously like a number of fox tails around his mantle, and hopefully you'll forgive me for seeing something faintly symbolic in this. The difficulty was deciding how to draw a Chinese butterfly. After studying a couple of butterfly paintings it soon appeared that Chinese artists are not overly concerned with a naturalistic representation and so I decided to make the insect a fantastic one. This was hardly settled when the Eight Immortals walked into my dreams. They were somewhat intoxicated and loudly demanded a place on paper. So a couple of sketches were made and then I woke, still a bit uncertain how to get the angle of Li's iron crutch right.

The way of heaven picture is based on the circulation of Ch'i within the body. Two acupuncture meridians are involved in the journey: Du Mai leads the Ch'i from the perineum along the back, following the spine up the body to the crown of the head and down the face to the mouth. Ren Mai leads Ch'i from the mouth down along the front of the body past the navel and the genitals to the perineum. Du Mai is the leading meridan (yang) and has 28 power points in traditional acupuncture, Ren Mai is the receiving meridan (yin) and has 24 points. Accordingly, DM is associated with fire and the sign Li, RM with cold water and the sign Kan. These trigrams refer to the forces that keep the Ch'i in motion in Taoist alchemy. In some schools of Taoism, regular visualizations are employed to ease this process. The rising and falling of the Ch'i can be visualized as the motion of a golden serpent (Chang Bo Tuan), as fire and water (Wei Boyang), as rising mists and falling rains (Yuyan) or as a continuous circuit of light, an image found in works attributed to Lü Tung Pin (See Wilhelm, *Secret of the Golden Flower*). What pictures you use is a matter of choice and efficiency. Dare to experiment if you really want to learn, or invent your own images. Keep in mind that all of these visualizations are aimed at a gentle and gradual transformation: the circulation of the Ch'i along the center line is experienced, but not enforced. A useful attitude is a friendly mood of joyousness. Other schools of Taoism advise that you do without visualization and focus on emptiness and effortless nondoing, knowing that the Ch'i will circulate much better when you don't bother to interfere with it. Alternate both methods if you like, depending on your mood and circumstances.

There are several trees in the pictures that were chosen because of their symbolism. Pines are a symbol for a long life or even immortality as they are so enduring and resistant against the cold. Plums, especially when they have blossoms, represent youth and potential and the first beginning of spring. Willows are closely associated with love and longing. Bamboo is not only essential for the survival of numerous Asian cultures, it can also be seen as a representation of the self-perfected human being as the stalks are hollow inside. The Lotus, rising from the muddy deep and emerging from water with its gorgeous flowers is a most common spiritual symbol that was popularized by the Buddhists.

The chart showing the symbols of the Eight Immortals around the trigrams of later heaven is based on a list given by Palmer. It is not the only possible way of assigning the Immortals to the Pa Kua, so you may enjoy to work out one or two different layouts. Its stimulating for the dear old brain. Better still, ask the Immortals when you meet them, and have a drink with them. Its worth it (so they say).

The banknote of hell is not one of my drawings. I wish I knew who had drawn it, so I could thank the artist.

The vision of Hsi Wang Mu is a blend of history with personal experience. The face you see is much like the one I saw, and so is the bizarre headdress, which is certainly not based on any historical image I know of. There are one or two classical shapes for Hsi Wang Mu's jade crown and hair-do, but rather than copy an original I preferred to draw the shape I saw her appear in - one shouldn't argue with deities, especially not about something as dull as an iconographic convention. While the face accords with subjective experience, the lay-out of the picture is based on a tile from the eastern Han period (25-220 CE) when the cult of this goddess was highly popular. The original image apparently graced the wall of a tomb in Qingbaixiang, Sichuan. It gives a rather dull looking portrait of the deity on her throne. This seat consists of somewhat abstract images of the green-blue dragon of the east and the white tiger of the west, sitting between them the goddess faces north. In usual Chinese custom, the seat of authority faces south and this raises a couple of interesting questions. For one thing, anyone looking at the tile is automatically in the authoritative seat with regard to the goddess. For another, if the goddess insists to gaze north in spite of social conventions, she must have a good reason for it. The three animals who play and dance at her feet are rather similar to the ones on the tile. They are the toad who dances in the moon, the three legged raven of the sun and the hare who collects the mushrooms of immortality (otherwise known as the tree of the three pearls). These mushrooms became a symbol of the K'un Lun mountains. Other beasts and beings on the tile were left out for reasons of space. Oh, and by the way, if you think that her eyes are empty, you are not looking at them in the proper state of mind.

Bibliography

Blofeld, John: *Taoism-the Quest for Immortality*, Allen & Unwin, London, 1979

Chen Zhao Fu: *China. Prähistorische Felsbilder*, Bär Verlag, Zürich 1989

Chuang Tsu, *Nan-hua chen ching, Inner Chapters*, transl. G.-F. Feng, Random House, New York 1974

----, *Reden und Gleichnisse des Tschuang-Tse*, transl. M. Buber, Manesse Verlag, Zürich, 1951

Cleary, Thomas (transl): *Practical Taoism*, Shambhala, Boston & London, 1996

----, *Vitality, Energy, Spirit. A Taoist Sourcebook*, Shambhala Publications, Boston, 1991

Creation of the Gods, transl. Gu Zhizhong, 2 volumes, New World Press, Beijing, 1992

Crowley, Aleister: *Tao Teh King*, Askin Publishers, London, 1976

Das alte China, Catalogue, Kunsthaus Zürich, 1996

Eberhard, Wolfram: *Lexikon chinesischer Symbole*, Diederichs Verlag, Köln 1983

Grinder, John and DeLozier, Judith: *Turtles All The Way Down-Prerequisites to Personal Genius*, (German) Junfermann, Paderborn, 1995

Heinze, Ruth-Inge: *Trance and Healing in Southeast Asia Today*, White Lotus Co. Bangkok, 1988

Hertzer, Dominique: *Das alte und das neue Yijing*, Diederichs Verlag, München 1996

----, *Das Mawangdui Yijing*, Diederichs Verlag, München, 1996

Hung Loh Mong, Der Traum der roten Kammer, transl. F. Kuhn, Insel Verlag, Frankfurt/M 1956

I Ching, or Book of Changes, especially the *Ta Chuan (Hsi Tz'u Chuan)*, transl. R. Wilhelm and Baynes, Routledge & Kegan Paul, London 1977

Kermadec, Jean-Michael de: *Lehrbuch der chinesischen Astrologie*, Ebertin Verlag, Freiburg 1983

Kwok Man Ho, Joanne O'Brian, Martin Palmer: *The Eight Immortals of Taoism*, Rider, London 1990

Lao Tsu, *Tao Teh Ching, The Book of the Way and its Virtue*, transl. J. J. L. Duyvendak, John Murray, London, 1954

Tao Te King, Nach den Seidentexten von Mawangdui, transl. H. G. Möller, Fischer Verlag, Frankfurt/M 1995

Lao-Tze's Tao-Teh-King, transl. Dr. Paul Carus, Open Court Publishing Company, Chicago, 1898

Li Gi, Das Buch der Riten, Sitten und Bräuche, transl. R. Wilhelm, Diederichs Verlag, München 1981

Liä Dsi, *Chong-xu-cheng-jing, Das wahre Buch vom quellenden Urgrund*, transl. Wilhelm, Diederichs Verlag, München 1967

Ling Meng-Chu: *Pai An King Ki, Chinesischer Liebesgarten*, transl. Tsung-Tung Chang, Erdmann Verlag, Herrenalb/Schwarzwald, 1964

Liu Hua Yang : *Hui-ming-ging, Das Buch von Bewußtsein und Leben*, transl. R. Wilhelm, in: *Das Geheimnis der goldenen Blüte*, Diederichs Verlag, Köln 1986

Li Yü: *Jou Pu Tuan*, transl. F. Kuhn, Verlag die Waage, Hamburg, 1965

Lü Bu We: Lü-shi ch'un-ch'iu, Frühling und Herbst des Lü Bu We, trans.Richard Wilhelm, Diederichs Verlag, Düsseldorf, 1971, 1979

Luo, Guanzhong & Feng, Menglong : *Pingyaozhuan, Der Aufstand der Zauberer*, transl. M. Porkert, Insel Verlag, Frankfurt/M 1986

Palastmuseum Peking, Schätze aus der Verbotenen Stadt, (ed.) Lothar Ledderose, Catalogue, Berliner Festspiele, Insel Verlag, Frankfurt/M, 1985

Palastmuseum Peking, *Schätze aus der verbotenen Stadt*, Catalogue, Insel Verlag, Frankfurt/M, 1985

Saso, Michael : *The Teachings of Taoist Master Chuang*, Yale University Press, New Haven and London 1978

Schätze Chinas in Museen der DDR. Catalogue, Staatl. Museen für Völkerkunde Dresden, Seemann Verlag, Leipzig 1989

Spare, Austin Osman, *The Witches' Sabbath, Axiomata*, Fulgur, London, 1992

Stockwell, Foster: *Religion in China Today*, New World Press, Beijing, 1993

Störig, Hans Joachim: *Kleine Weltgeschichte der Philosophie*, Kohlhammer Verlag, Stuttgart, 1950

T'ai-i-chin-hua-tsung-chih, transl. R. Wilhelm, B. Hendrischke, in: *Das Geheimnis der goldenen Blüte*, Diederichs Verlag, Köln 1986

Tannahill, Reay: *Sex in History*, Sphere Books, London, 1981

Topping, Audrey: *China's incredible Find*, National Geographic, April 1978

Trungpa, Chogyam: *The Heart of the Buddha*, Shambhala Publications, Boston, 1991

Meditation in Action, Stuart & Watkins, London, 1969

Walls, Jan & Yvonne: *Classical Chinese Myths*, Joint Publishing Co. Hong Kong 1984

Wei Boyang: *Cantong Qi*, as *The Secret of Everlasting Life*, transl. and commentary R. Bertschinger, Element, Shaftesbury 1994, German edition, transl. from the English and Chinese, I. Fischer-Schreiber, Krüger Verlag, Frankfurt/M, 1997

Wege der Götter und Menschen, Religionen im traditionellen China, (ed.) Claudius Müller, Wu Shun-chi, Catalogue, Museum für Völkerkunde Berlin, Reimer Verlag, Berlin, 1989

Wilhelm, Hellmut : *Sinn des I Ging*, Diederichs Verlag

Wilhelm, Richard: *Chinesische Märchen*, Diederichs Verlag, München 1958

Wong, Eva: *Teachings of the Tao*, Shambhala, Boston & London, 1997

Wu Ch'eng En : *Monkey*, transl. Waley, Allen & Unwin, London (*The Journey to the West*)

Yuan Mei: *Chinesische Geistergeschichten*, Insel Verlag Frankfurt/M, 1997 (*What Confucius Did Not Mention*)

Zheng, Chantal : *Mythen des alten China*. Diederichs Verlag, München 1990

Index

Other Titles by Jan Fries

Helrunar -A Manual of Rune Magick

This book is a complete manual of magick based upon the arcane symbolism and secret techniques known as the runes. The runes are for all! - they are not a new religion or 'folkish' claptrap but a vibrant magical system that really works! *'...eminently practical and certainly breaks new ground.'* - Ronald Hutton (author *Pagan Religions of the Ancient British Isles*)
350pp 1869928199, £9.99/$19.99, 100 ill.

Visual Magick - A manual of freestyle shamanism

It shows how magicians, witches, artists and therapists can improve visionary abilities, enhance imagination, activate the inner senses, and discover new modes of Trance awareness. The emphasis is on direct experience and the reader is asked to think, act, do, and enjoy as s/he wills.
136pp 1869928180 £7.99$14.99

Seidways -Shaking, Swaying and Serpent Mysteries

Seething is probably the most useful magical technique I have ever learned. I first was taken by the pleasure of it. My body felt warm and sensual, and seething in the hips felt quite sexual. I liked the feeling of my body taking over where the shaking was first voluntary - but I could still have some control, making the shaking stronger or more subtle. After a while I started to see visions - something that very rarely happens to me. I could see (with my physical eyes, not astrally!) the surface of the land in the centre of the circle rippling, like waves of energy. It was a really moving experience in a site that - until then - had not been particularly 'special' to me... it ..has had a major impact upon my magical work which used to be largely indoors, as at last I have found a way that I can work outdoors. This gives my magical work a potency that it simply didn't have before. - Shantidevi in chapter twelve 'Rhythms and the Mind'
350pp 1869928-369 48 ills £10.99/$20

Available worldwide (ask your bookseller to order from New Leaf or Weisers). For information about other distributors, direct sales: Mandrake of Oxford, PO Box 250, Oxford, OX1 1AP (UK) tel +44 1865 243671, fax +44 1865 432929. If you are connected to the internet you can email us on mandrake@mandrake.cix.co.uk or search for Janfries on various search engines.

Siddha Quest for Immortality.

Sexual, alchemical and medical secrets of the Tamil Siddhas, the *Poets of the Powers*

By Professor Kamil V Zvelebil.

In South India there is a society where priests and lay people claim supernatural powers. Where a sophisticated medical system underlies a quest for physical longevity and psychic immortality. And where arcane and sexual rituals take place that are far removed from the Brahmanic tradition of the rest of India.

That society is the Tamil Siddhas. **In the Siddha Quest for Immortality** world Tamil expert K Zvelebil offers a vivid picture of these people: their religious beliefs, their magical rites, their alchemical practices, their complex system of medicine, and their inspired tradition of poetry.

Topics covered include: .On Siddhas Medicine./The Ideological Basis of Siddhas Quest of Immortality./Basic Tenets of Siddhas Medicine./Diseases and Their Cure./ Yoga in Siddhas Tradition./Daily Regime./Siddhas Alchemy./Rejuvenation, Longevity, and 'Immortality'./Doctrines and Traditions of the Siddhas./Tantrik Siddhas and Siddhas Attitudes to Sex./Siddhas Poetry and Other Texts. ISBN 1 869928 431. Price £9.99/$20

If you have access to the internet and would like to read a short extract, point your browser at http://www.cix.co.uk/~mandrake/siddha.htm